AUDIENCES across the country
have laughed, pondered, shrugged,
agreed, considered, analyzed and
been made to think
as Ethel Barrett romped through
the basics of psychology and logic,
so carefully wrapped in hilarious anecdotes
that the didactics are scarely recognized.

Over and over, the reaction of those
who listened was, "I laughed so hard,
I forgot to take notes.
Can I get a copy?
You said so much that I would like
to think about."
At last the answer is "yes."
Here is your copy!
Read it . . . laugh . . . think.

We would worry
less about what
others think of us,
if we realized how
seldom they do.

DON'T LOOK NOW

by Ethel Barrett

G/L
REGAL
BOOKS
TM

A Division of G/L Publications
Glendale, California, U.S.A.

Over 80,000 in print

Second Printing, 1969

Third Printing, 1970

Fourth Printing, 1971

© Copyright 1968 by G/L Publications

Printed in U.S.A.

Published by

Regal Books Division, G/L Publications

Glendale, California, U.S.A.

Library of Congress Catalog Card No. 68-25807

ISBN 0-8307-0019-6

To Priscilla Ann,
                who gets along with everybody.*

*As far as I know.

Contents

Foreword

This book is a compilation of a series of talks given at Leadership Training conferences and college chapels throughout the country.

When I was asked to write it, I demurred at first. But the more I thought of it the more attractive the idea became. For writing this kind of book does us psychologists—amateur and otherwise—no end of good. We can examine our own faults and problems and go over our own mistakes objectively as if they were *yours*.

What a jolly idea.

After talking ourselves through a couple of hundred pages the therapy is complete. We have cajoled, scolded and encouraged ourselves, and have gotten ourselves up by the scruff of the neck, so to speak, and all the while pretending it is *you* who needs straightening out.

It is admittedly a sneaky way to do it. But if everybody benefits, where's the harm? I could find nothing but mutual good.

God is, of course, the answer to every problem. But the better we can see and face ourselves the more he has to work with. The talks were given and the book is written on this premise. But with a touch of laughter, holding the pen lightly.

If you cannot look upon yourself with some amusement, this little book is not the fare for you.

Humanly speaking . . .

THE HARDEST thing to give is in. The caption under a man-wife cartoon with the wife saying, *"We're* not incompatible—*you're* incompatible" is funny on first thought, and contains more—much more than a soupçon of truth on second.

And the easiest person to fool is one's self. If nothing else, humanly speaking, has proved it, the medical profession has. For decades doctors have known that they could treat many patients successfully for real or imagined ailments by a little therapeutic hanky-panky. Placebos, in brightly colored capsules or bitter pills or a bitter tincture, prescribed solemnly and with proper authority, have brought about improvement in more ailments than this world dreams of. And to add to our humiliation, these bogus pills have not only effected a cure,

15

but have actually created some of the adverse "side effects" of the drug they were imitating. Some patients have complained of trembling, dry mouth, vomiting, stomach pain and even skin rashes after taking pills that have no more power than a dud firecracker.

Deceiving ourselves is the greatest talent we have. Taking ourselves too seriously is the greatest trap we can fall into. Learning to chuckle at ourselves is the most potent weapon we can possess. For, stripped of glamour, appearances, our "image," and other various and sundry cumbersome accoutrements, we are really a sorry lot. And the sooner we realize it, and clear away the trappings, the sooner God can get to work on us.

Getting along with people doesn't just happen; it has to be worked for. In the college department of Hollywood Presbyterian church, a girl stood up in prayer meeting during testimony time and said, "I had a French exam last Friday and I had so many things to do all week and I worried about that exam so—"

Dr. Henrietta Mears, who was sitting a row ahead, folded her arms and thrust her head forward and downward sharply, chin on chest, an indication that she was either very thoughtful or very displeased.

"But I asked the Lord to help me," the girl went on, "and the week went by and I said, 'Lord you're just going to have to help me—'"

Miss Mears shifted in her seat. "Well I hope you did a little studying, too," she muttered to herself.

Yes. The least we can do is our homework.

Begin at
the beginning

THIS REALLY should be a book on how to get along well in *family relationships*, for on this subject I am an expert. My family life is serene and problem-free; there are no strained feelings, no personality conflicts, no conflicts over money, no problems over give-and-take, and there has not been an argument or a voice raised in anger in years. I am absolutely on top of it all and above such things.

I live alone.*

I am paterfamilias, materfamilias, keeper of the exchequer, maker of all decisions, and undisputed monarch. And that's enough to make a saint out of

*I am a widow, my children have long since flown the nest, (now we have just neat little visits, all fun and frolic) and because of extensive travel, there is not even a dog to question the fact that I am the absolute boss around here, and no mistake.

19

any virago. My twenty-twenty hindsight is absolutely phenomenal on family relationships, and I know every answer in the book. I didn't *then*. But I do *now*.

The old axiom that "solitude is often the best company" is true if we heed the word "often" (or even change it to "sometimes") and don't take solitude across the board as the answer to everything. For in solitude we can develop everything but character. We can achieve much learning, stuff our heads with theory, learn the art of meditation and yes, even become so spiritual that our countenance is blessed with "the fixed ethereal sweet smile of bad religious art everywhere"—but it is only by bumping into other people that we develop character.

And you just can't go around bumping into other people without getting chipped and bruised.

Now I loathe statistics and theory because every time I come across a generality and get a nice comfortable pat answer to something, I immediately come across a dozen exceptions to the rule. Because I'm always coming across *people*, and they have a disconcerting way of upsetting theory.

But statistics tell us (and there is a plethora of statistics on the subject) that people fail in jobs, in marriage, in careers, or whatever, and that roughly 60% of them fail because they cannot get along with *other* people.

Here is a young lady applying for a job. With a singular lack of imagination we shall call her Miss "X." She is neatly and attractively dressed. She has poise and presence. She is formidably efficient and eminently qualified for the job. But the personnel director has her job history on his desk, and although there seems to be a different reason why she was discharged from each job in the past, there is a pattern there, and he is sharp enough to see it. She does not get the job.

Or take Mr. "Z." He is being told that "perhaps he might be happier someplace else." He is also eminently qualified for his job. But the same pattern is there. He cannot get along with other people. This appalling pattern follows these poor wretches all their lives, from job to job, through marriage, or through celibacy, or whatever their human relationships might be, and plagues them to the end. And it's repeated in the lives of untold thousands.

Secular business is concerned enough about it to spend millions to send their junior executives dashing off to take courses on human relations. There *must* be something to it.

There is.

"Ah," we say, "but we are Christians. We are working in the *church*. The physical church and the spiritual church. And the only people we have to get along with are the pastor and the assistant pastor (or pastors) and the choir director and the Christian education director and the board of education and the board of deacons and all the other boards and the president of the women's guild and the Sunday School superintendents and the Sunday School teachers and the congregation and all the committees and—"

Yes.

Whoever we are and in whatever position and whomever we bump into we have the same problem. Much of Christian work is volunteer labor and nobody gets discharged. But sixty percent of us are blowing our gaskets over something most of the time because of the same problem. We cannot get along with people.

What's wrong?

Let's go back to some basic fundamentals. Not to learn them. You already know them. Let's review them. Let's go back to the time when you didn't have to work to get along with anybody.

You are in a basket.

You are in a basket.

The first thing you notice is the quilted padding on the side. And then the rattle tied to the top with a ribbon, all in a bow, just for you. And then there is the ruffle. Dotted Swiss, with unbleached muslin underneath to give it body, and if you have any sense at all you figure that material for a good ruffle has to be one and a half times the circumference—so there's dotted Swiss at $1.89 a yard and unbleached muslin at 79¢ a yard—and it's about, roughly, three yards around that basket—

Well!

That's quite an investment, right there, and to add to that, there's all that attention. All you have to do is smile, which you know is just a gas grimace, but everyone else thinks is a smile, and everyone rushes to hover over you and exclaim and you have it made without even turning a hair.

Well you know the rest. In a matter of weeks, you become devious. If they don't hover over you, you cry "Pin!" or "Gas!" And you know better, but they don't, and you get plomped over somebody's back and whomped on *your* back, and fussed over until you're satisfied that you are "king of the road" and don't let anybody ever forget it.

Then you find your hand and count your fingers and stick them in your mouth and then you find your feet and count your toes and stick *them* in your mouth and everybody exclaims as if you'd done something absolutely phenomenal and then you exude peculiar sounds that are dubbed "crowing"—and you've been crowing ever since.

Then you begin to grow up a little. You develop in different areas. And some of them are easy.

Take muscular coordination. All things being equal you can take it as a matter of course. You learn to spin a top. You learn that you must wind the string around the top—just so—and then—zing! Pull it and off it goes spinning, just as you knew it would. Your muscular coordination is developing very well, thank you.

But then a shadow falls across the nursery. It's one of those "adults."

"Share the top with Susan," it says.

You wind the string around again. "I don't want

23

to share the top with Susan," you say matter-of-factly, your old "id" welling up. But the adult is beaming with strange theories you know not of.

"But we *love* to share our things, don't we?" it says.

Well *that's* a new one.

And before you have time to recover, it says, "We love our friends. And we love *Susan*, don't we?"

"I don't even *like* Susan," you say, deciding to go whole-hog and straighten this out at once. Actually this last remark is off the top of your head because you have never thought the matter through before. The idea of loving anybody to the point of sharing is something beyond the pale of your experience and too appalling to comprehend. Share! What will these adults think of next? Monstrous!

But you pit your pristine logic against the adults' more sophisticated logic in vain. You are too unevenly matched; the contest is grossly unfair. It winds up with a smarting whack on your wrist and you discover to your dismay that you love Susan and you love your friends and you love to share your things whether you like it or not.

Or take the matter of identifying objects. It too is a snap. And very rewarding. There is no other area where you can get as much applause and approbation. Somebody gives you a carpenter's kit for Christmas. "Hammer!" you say, picking it up. "Oh see the hammer!" they cry with squeals and knowing looks at each other, indicating how smart you are. "Saw!" You try again. This is working out very well. "Saw!" they shout, beside themselves. But then you go over and whomp grandpa on the shin

24

with the hammer and try sawing up the piano bench and the whole wretched business repeats itself and you discover that you not only adore sharing, you also restrain yourself from hurting people and destroying property.

But before you can get your thoughts organized and perfect your defensive tactics, indeed, before you can say "Tell and Show" your mother has you by one chubby hand and is dragging you off to school.

"This," you think optimistically, "is going to be different." Clean slate, fresh start, and all that sort of thing.

But you run amuck almost at once. "Now we are all going to be flowers," the teacher says, her face a study in beneficence. Then she waves her arms over her head. "And we're going to stand and wave our leaves in the breeze." Everybody does.

"And we're going to turn our faces to the sun—" Without losing the radiant smile, she eyes you and hisses softly, "Don't do that."

"And we're going to nod our—(Don't do that, darling)—nod our heads in the—(because I said *not* to, darling, that's why.)"

Now, we are all going to be flowers..

All your instincts tell you to hang on to your pants.

25

You comply, though you cannot fathom her logic, for waving your leaves in the breeze when your pants are falling down is no mean feat. All your instincts tell you to hang onto your pants.

You've run into that frightening adult logic again.

I remember running into it my very first day in school. We each had a large square of brown wrapping paper in front of us and the teacher beamed at us and told us in a high trilly voice that in a moment we were going to pick it up. And we were going to pick it up ever so carefully and *quietly* because "we know," she said archly, picking up hers and rattling it, "that brown—paper—*talks!*"

She was really quite coy about it, but her charm was lost on me. Actually she lost me at that precise moment, for I reasoned that any idiot ought to know that brown paper does not talk, and I eyed her with a jaundiced eye for the rest of the term.

The dreadful truth does not come to everyone in the same way, but, one way or another, you are brought up with a jolt. You have entered organized society. This is going to be a grim business, a grim business indeed.

Muscular coordination was easy. Sharing was rough. Identifying objects was easy. Refraining from hurting people and destroying property was rough. Learning to live with "don't do that" was rough. Entering organized society was shattering. All of these things dealt a great blow to your pristine mind and atavistic propensities.

Developing physically (all things being equal) is a cinch compared with developing emotionally.

26

Anyhow, somewhere along this hazardous road you became a Christian. You may have been nurtured in the Christian faith from babyhood, "carried out of Egypt" in your mother's arms. And when the proper time for you came, you overtly accepted what you had known and believed in your heart all along.

Or perhaps you were not nurtured in the faith, but grew up "outside the camp." Then your decision made a dramatic change in your life and dumped you into an entirely new set of people and into another world.

If, with you, it was the latter, then your naivete and vulnerability are almost too painful to contemplate. Your disenchantment with people will be as explosive and dramatic and intense as your conversion was. If, with you, it was the former, then you already knew.

Christians are human beings.

In either case you were confronted with the living God in the person of the Lord Jesus Christ, and now many of your human-relation problems will be in the church and with Christians.

And your childhood is behind you. You are now an adult. Well, you are more or less an adult. Actually you are an adult in some areas and less adult than you think, in others.

Are you scrapping with the world, always fighting the controls? ("Well they might introduce that closely-graded curriculum in our Sunday School but I am not going to teach it in my fifth grade. I'm going to teach what I please. And this teachers' training is perfect nonsense. I'm willing to

27

teach but I will not be relegated to meetings and all the rest of it.") In this particular area you are about fourteen—testing your "grown-upness."

Do you cry to get your way? In this area you are still under six.

Do you find it difficult to admit you are wrong? Do you blame others for your mistakes? You're a nice average four.

Do you lock up your supplies, guard your tools and accoutrements? Can't bear to share your visual aids? You're about two and a half.

Are you bossy and domineering? You'd better hurry, children begin to grow out of that one around six.

In some area or another, you're either impossible or a great big lovable kid, depending upon who is appraising you.

Many of us have not come as far from our childhood as we think.

I was riding on a plane to Atlanta once, with a charming little girl. Well I wasn't exactly with the little girl—she sort of spilled over on to me from across the aisle where her young mother sat with a one-year-old baby. The little mother looked tired and worn and the baby was restless, and before the law of self-preservation had set in, I offered to take care of the little girl, is what actually happened.

She had a coloring book. I had a Bible story book. Her mother had some candy. And there was a water dispenser with dixie cups dead ahead. So with these provisions we started out on our journey. First she colored a bit of Shadrach Meshach and Abednego. Then I read her a story. Then we looked at the scenery below. Then she had some candy. Then she wanted a drink. Then I read her another story. Then she had some more candy. Then she had some *more* candy. Then she wanted a drink. Then her stomach felt squeamish and we went to the lounge. Then she wanted a drink. Then she colored some more of Shadrach Meshach and Abednego and then we read some more and then she had more candy and then we went to the lounge and then she wanted a drink and then we looked at more scenery and then she wanted a drink and then we went to the lounge and then she colored more of Shadrach Meshach and Abednego and then we had a story and then we went to the lounge and then we looked at the scenery which was at long last the runway and then we landed.

I said goodbye to the grateful little family with mixed feelings, half of which are too unspiritual to describe here, and hurried away to the ticket counter to discover that my connecting plane was three hours late. When you travel a great deal, common sense dictates that you relax and take set-backs philosophically, so I found a comfortable corner and settled down with a book I'd been anxious to read, heady with the relief and exhilaration of being back in the mature adult world with which I was more familiar.

Well, first I read awhile. Then I wandered around the airport and looked at the scenery. Then I discovered some Pralines. Now I don't ordinarily eat candy while traveling, but good Pralines are hard to come by, so I bought a box, and sampled some. Then I was thirsty so I wandered over to a water dispenser and got a drink. Then I read some more of my book. Then I had some more Pralines. Then I had some *more* Pralines. Then I wanted a drink. Then, as I am unaccustomed to candy while traveling, my stomach felt squeamish and I went to the lounge. Then I wanted a drink. Then I read some more of my book and then I sneaked a teensy nibble of Praline and then I went to the lounge and then I wanted a drink and then I wandered around the airport and looked at more scenery and then I wanted a drink and then I went to the lounge and then I read some more of my book and then I went to the lounge and then I looked at the scenery and at long last my plane was announced and I ran for it. And then it suddenly struck me that in my own mature adult world I had done everything the little girl had done except color Shadrach Meshach and Abednego.

If you are adult and emotionally mature in every area it will be in somebody else's opinion; you will be the last one to suspect it. If even Paul had his doubts, who are we to boast?

So let's go on the assumption that we are *not* mature in some areas, that we do need help, that there is something we can learn, and get on with it.

It is not necessary to take the fabric of our lives and turn it inside out and probe morbidly "where the threads are knotted and the loose ends hang" for our purposes here.

There are some rules, some of them unbelievably simple, that can change our lives. And make bumping into other people practically painless.

Two little words

THE TERM "bumping into people" is a rather salty analogy but actually a very practical one, for in this business of getting along with people the first big fundamental fact we have to contend with, is

FRICTION

According to the laws of mechanics or physics, friction is the resistance of a surface to the relative motion, as sliding or rolling, of a body moving along a given surface. In the dictionary, the word "friction" is followed by the words friction clutch, friction drive, friction gearing, friction head, friction layer, friction match, friction pile, friction saw, friction tape.

So two or more objects coming together is always accompanied by friction. This is most dramatically

33

demonstrated in machinery. You can find it out the easy way by just believing it, or you can neglect adding oil to your car until it is all gone, and find out the hard way that the law of friction is an indisputable fact.

You find out the hard way that the law of friction is an indisputable fact.

And so it is in the realm of human-relations. When two or more personalities come together, there is friction. Anywhere from barely perceptible, when small differences cause no problems at all, to "My, when they're together you can almost see the sparks fly!"

The crux is to determine where you are in the machinery. Are you a chief? Are you an Indian? You'll soon find out which ones you are working for, which ones are working for you, which ones you are working with, and which ones you would just as soon do without; your business is to see that there is no one you are working *against*. Your relationship to others depends upon your position in the machinery and the smartest thing you can do is to find it and stay there, with a minimum amount of friction.

One person who has been appointed to teach a Sunday School class or be on a church decorating committee and winds up wanting to dictate the church policies and the pastor's sermons and decide where the mission money should go, can give a church a bad case of vapor lock for years, and though my mechanical know-how reached its peak when I learned to fill a stapler, I understand that vapor lock is a hot-air bubble that causes a blockage in the fuel line.

When I first went to the coast to work for Gospel Light Publications I asked myself some questions for my own edification. I cannot remember exactly what they were now; I do remember that they were couched in discreet circumlocution, gentle humility and great spirituality.

1. Did they want me to share in their great ministry? (Did they want me to look over the organization, pick out various and sundry weaknesses that might come to my attention and point them out.)

2. Did they want me to assume responsibility? (Did they want me to take over in any area where I thought I knew it all and tell everyone how to run it my way.)

3. Did they want me to be helpful above and beyond the call of duty? (Did they want me to worry about whether other people were doing their jobs that were none of my business, or work odd hours overtime and let everybody know about it loud and clear.)

4. Did they want me to be resourceful? (Did they want me to find devious means of getting

my own way when I was crossed or blocked.)

5. Did they want me to have discernment? (Did they want me to have a knack for sniffing out other people's faults and failures and reporting them.)

6. Did they want me to contribute? (Did they want me to force my ideas on everyone and go off whining and complaining if they did not accept them unconditionally, giving me carte blanche to carry them out.)

Well it turned out they did want me to share in the ministry, assume responsibility, be helpful and resourceful, have discernment and to contribute. It was my responsibility to do so from my own place in the machinery and within bounds. And I reasoned that if God set bounds for the mighty ocean, who was I to quibble?

Actually I discovered that ideas and frank opinions from *everyone* were not only tolerated but encouraged and acted upon, and how this has been done down through the years without blowing up Colorado Boulevard I cannot explain outside the fact that everyone manages to stay in his own place in the machinery.

So in human relations as in solid matter, friction is a fact. But in human relations, statistics show that 90% of all friction is superficial. No matter how your own personal problem with friction is giving you blisters, the experts are against you, nation-wide analyses are against you; you have only a 10% chance of proving your case is serious.

If it is true, that most friction is superficial, then clearly, we should not bother our heads about it.

36

"Ignore it and it will go away." Unfortunately, that is not as easy to do in practice as it is to realize in theory. Not because we do not see it's the sensible thing to do, but because of the way we are made. The Chinese proverb, "There are as many worlds as there are men; each lives alone within his own," is all too true, and we have the unhappy knack of taking everything personally. Rather like the little town of Rome, Texas, that telegraphed to the League of Nations in 1935 that, lest there be any confusion on the subject, it should be made clear that it was Rome, Italy, not Rome, Texas, that had launched the invasion of Ethiopia!

The penchant for taking everything personally is here to stay. No matter how many times we squash it, it crops up again in unguarded moments, so we may as well learn to live with it. In this connection, it is well to remember the second little word

TEMPORARY

Behavior is dynamic, not static, and nobody is going to be precisely the same next week, or even tomorrow, as he was today. He may think he is and you may think he is, but it simply is not so. For we get experience with every move we make, whether we know it or not. The Chinese have a handy proverb for this, too: "Experience is something we get while we are looking for something else." For though experience is the actual living through an event, it is also the effect upon the judgment or feelings produced by personal and direct impressions. And so we change even while we think we are doing nothing.

Psychiatrists have carved our personalities up into neat little packages. And to add to the confusion we do not necessarily fit neatly into *one* of them—we may be a combination of more than one. Now one of those packages is called the "cycloid" personality. That's the one that is like a Yo-Yo—it goes up and down, and if a cycloid goes over the border line into insanity he becomes a manic-depressive, sometimes so hysterically wound up he talks himself hoarse, and sometimes so deep in depression he can only sit and stare and is unable to even feed himself.

But no matter which kind of personality we happen to have, we *all* have a bit of the cycloid in us. We have what we call the cyclothymic curve. Our moods go up and down, and no two people's curve is precisely the same. It has nothing to do with sex or age. Men have it. Women have it. Boys and girls have it. Carnal Christians have it. Spiritual Christians have it.

The "plunges" may come every few weeks, or every few months, or once a year, or whatever; everyone is blessed with, or stuck with, his own cycle, as the case may be. Some people plunge way down and are despondent and withdrawn. Some are just touchy. Some are aggressively irritable. And some, bless their hearts, just seem to stay on an even keel, their little plunges barely perceptible; they would hardly make a quiver on a graph. They are the ones who discourage us.

I knew one once. She was always smiling. It was one of those dimpled smiles that simply never came off. If you asked her how she was and everything

38

was fine, it was so eminently fine that her whole face broke up into little pieces and quivered with delight. She could somehow mouth every consonant and vowel in the English language without ever changing that smile or losing those dimples. If you asked her how she was and everything was wrong, you got the bad news through that same smile. The direst of circumstances would not, could not wipe it off. It occurred to me once that she could even ring somebody's door bell and sing out bravely through that smile, "I just ran over your dog." Perhaps the day that occurred to me, *my* cyclothymic curve was down. It *was* an unworthy thought.

So we are stuck with our cyclothymic curves. We can't eliminate them, but it is helpful just to know they are there; it takes the sting out.

It is even better to chart them. Notice when the plunges come, and mark your calendar. It might take awhile, but eventually a pattern will emerge, and you will be ready for the wretched plunges when they arrive. It saves a lot of futile hand-wringing, wondering why everything is going wrong.

But the epitome of success in this exercise is to chart the curves of *other* people, too. People you live with, work with, socialize with. It takes a bit of doing, but it's well worth it. For once you have their cycle charted in your little notebook, you have a formidable defence when they descend upon you in one of their plunges. It gives you an aplomb and a composure and a sense of being on top of it all, that is really quite heady.

And it gives you a new realization of the word

39

"temporary." When your Sunday School superintendent comes raging into your department and bites your head off, instead of thinking, "Every Sunday he comes in here and bites my head off," you simply consult your little notebook, mark him off and think, "Well, that's that. The old boy isn't due to bite my head off again for another five weeks."

But more important, instead of thinking he's an ogre, you find yourself sighing in sympathy, knowing full well that it is only a matter of time (and you consult your little book again) and you'll be in for it, too.

What to do about friction that is a result of "off days"? Disregard it. Don't "simmer." Don't be "hurt." Don't "talk it out." Don't talk about it to others. And don't worry about it. It's TEMPORARY. It's not personal. And it's probably not serious.

This "temporary" theory is tricky, for sometimes it's a long-range affair, and if you don't watch yourself it can trip you up.

I got involved in the life of a little boy once, and

40

a happy and riotous involvement it was. It was also a frustrating involvement, sometimes to the point of distraction. His name was Richard, and he descended upon us like a tornado, coming home from school one day with my two sons—very much the second-grader, and yet somehow prodigiously old. His mother worked and he had nowhere to go until five o'clock. He had an aura of failure about him but he never seemed to recognize it, for he lived a great roaring life in his own fantasy, and shared it with us freely, doling out great chunks of daring-do at the drop of a hat. Everything reminded him of some great possession he had or some phenomenal feat he had performed. He rode the range, he went to sea, he traveled the world. His imagination was fantastic. We prodded him gently on the difference between fact and fantasy, but we enjoyed him vastly. I felt guilty sometimes at the unworthy thought that if he ever reformed, life would be dull indeed.

I told him about the wonderful love of God, about the Lord Jesus, about the good news that this living God wanted *him* for a son. I took him to Vacation Bible School, I took him to Sunday School, but all this good news somehow escaped him and he remained impervious to everything he heard. After spending the morning at VBS or Sunday School getting all straightened out, he would hop off our home-going bus, (after I'd paid the fare and before the driver had had a chance to close the door) and we would all scramble off, too, and chase him madly up the alley between the downtown theatre and the department store.

I kept vowing that I never wanted to see Richard again, but see him I did. He was in my blood and we were inextricably chained together by some curious rapport that I could neither fathom nor deny. The denouement came when we had to move to another town. My feelings toward Richard were ambivalent. I loved him and I couldn't stand him, all at the same time. And I wept over leaving him.

The little story might have ended there except that I couldn't bear to just walk off and leave it unfinished with him dangling like a deserted participle, so I went to a woman in the church whom I knew was a great prayer-warrior, and asked her to pray for this little boy she had never met. We covenanted to pray together.

Ten months later I received a letter from her out of the blue and the impossible (humanly speaking) had happened. Richard's mother had started bringing him to Sunday School, and stayed herself. Then his father. And the following Sunday they were all going to be baptized. They had accepted Christ and were joining the church. I crumpled the letter up next to my heart and wept all over it. Dear little Richard!

Eight years later I went back to that church to speak. My prayer-warrior came up to me afterward, and said, "Would you like to say hello to Richard?"

Ah, little Richard! Indeed I would.

Tears welled up within me as I followed her through the crowd, anticipating this joyous reunion with my little cherub. Several people somehow got between us when she found him, and I heard her voice: "Richard, would you like to say hello to Mrs.

Barrett?" And this flip fifteen-year-old monster replied, imitating her voice with deadly accuracy, "No, I wouldn't like to say hello to Mrs. Barrett."

I would have fled if possible, but the people melted away and there I was, face to face with a giant of a boy who shook hands awkwardly and murmured something unintelligible with great embarrassment and made his escape before I could muster my faculties.

I remained smiling and bloody but unbowed, but inside I wailed, "Oh Richard, you fiend, you breaker of Good Samaritans' hearts, you *ingrate!*" And then I thought, "well what did you expect, in the name of common sense, what *did* you expect?"

I expected time to stand still is what I expected, and I didn't even have the grace to blush for shame, so nonplused was I at the moment. I'd forgotten that all things are temporary, even on a long-range basis. There was nothing wrong with Richard except that he was fifteen, and he was doing par-for-the-course.

This should have been enough to straighten me out, but if there is one thing I'm consistent in, it's that I never learn anything so, of course, I did it again.

This time it was a young woman. She came to me without a job and without a Saviour and very very broke, materially and spiritually. I introduced her to Christ, gave her some clothes and a wee bit of money, and by some miracle I had a contact that landed her a job as a clerk in a department store. I blessed her and prayed with her and sent her on her way. And I felt so noble I could hardly stand it.

Two years later she phoned me. She'd made out well, was now a buyer of women's clothing in another city. She was just passing through. Did I want to have lunch? I did. I could hardly wait to hear her outpourings of gratitude and to give her some more encouragement, peppered with my wisdom and counsel.

The jolt came when I met her in a downtown restaurant. She had more money on her back in one outfit than I could afford to spend in a year. We sat down. She pulled off her kid gloves. I pulled off my cotton gloves. She looked at me, wide-eyed, and said, "Hasn't the Lord been wonderful?"

Full-blown, into my mind it came. All at once, and more quickly than it can be told. "What do you mean, the Lord? *Me* and the Lord. I gave you money. I found you a job. I, I, I—" Horrors. I gave *that* to the Lord at once in the same flash with which it had come to me, and I am more ashamed of it than of many more heinous crimes I've committed. Telling about it takes a paragraph; actually it was only a twinge. But the implications of that twinge are horrendous!

I honestly rejoiced over her success, but I wanted our relationship to be on the same basis it had been two years before! Me the Great White Mother. Her the underling. Me the hierophant. Her the neophyte. I had forgotten the all-things-are-temporary—even on-a-long-range-basis rule.

We cannot leave a person or a situation or a relationship or a class or a ministry or a post and go back years or even months later and expect to find it just the same. It is the law of dynamics.

**If you're not
getting along . . .**

IF WE ARE NOT getting along with someone, naturally we want to do something about it. Being on bad terms with another is sinful, contrary to our precepts, and shamefully out of character—our Christian character. And besides it is not very jolly. It is nerve-wracking, energy-consuming, and upsetting to the tranquillity of our lives. All the wrong gastric juices flow, our blood pressure goes up; in short, it's a nuisance.

Now the Christian thing to do, is take it to the Lord. And most of us do, in all good faith. We ask the Lord to forgive that wretched virago, or that Simon Legree, or that nosy Miss Marple, or that purveyor of mischief, or whatever the case may be. Or some of us are even more spiritual and instead, ask the Lord to forgive that poor unfortunate mixed-up saint. In either case we get up from our knees serene and thankful that everything is going to be all right just as soon as the Lord straightens the other fellow out. We ask God for patience to bear it in the meantime, of course, as good Christians should.

The chosen few of us (the *really* spiritual ones) even ask the Lord to show us if anything is wrong in *ourselves* to have whipped up this messy little discord. Usually it's a nice general statement, like the "Lord, send us revival and let it begin in me" sort of thing. It's very sincere, very earnest, and also very safe. It skirts neatly around details, circumvents anything specific, and leaves us comfortable and refreshed in the fact that we have honestly tried to do *our* part. Let the other fellow beware!

If you are not getting along with someone, here are some things you can do. It's not the whole answer (a searching by the Holy Spirit is the whole answer, and you can help by being honest) but it's good for a starter.

Examine your own personality with brutal frankness. I was skidding downtown in the rain early one Sunday morning, to do a radio program, when I spotted a little boy and a man, evidently his father, at a bus stop. I recognized the little boy as one who, with his brother, waited for the school bus with my sons. So I stopped and rolled down my window.

"If you're headed for downtown, get in!" I called.

They were. They were indeed going to the Mother Science church not far from my studio. They got in, dripping and grateful, and off we started. Just to start a conversation, I turned to the lad and said, "Can't your brother come to Sunday School today?" "Nope," he said promptly, "he's got poison ivy."

"Paulie," his father said evenly, "your brother

48

does not have poison ivy. It's an error of mind."

"My that's too bad," I said, feeling mischievous and throwing caution to the winds.

"I've got some, too," offered Paulie, "but it's not as bad as his."

"Paulie!" said his father, this time not so evenly. "You do *not* have poison ivy. It's an error of thinking."

"Where's *yours*?" I asked brightly, entering into the spirit of the thing.

"*Paul*," said his father, leaving off the "ie" to indicate that things had gone far enough and there was to be no more nonsense. "You do *not*. Tell Mrs. Barrett that you do not have poison ivy."

And Paulie came up with a classic. "Mrs. Barrett," he said, "I do not have poison ivy. It is an error of thinking." Then he dived at his arm with eager fingernails. "But it sure itches!" he wailed.

Examine your own personality with brutal frankness. If you have poison ivy of the personality you may deny it but it is still there. Don't look now but your poison ivy is itching!

If you are not getting along with someone, it might be a good idea to determine *who* isn't getting along with *whom*.

I hauled my two sons off to a Christian psychologist one time when they were in their teens. The reason was obvious. They had become singularly uncommunicative, sullen and spunky, and were trying in every way not to get along with me.

"Give these kids tests!" I cried. "They're not getting along with me!"

"We'll *all* take tests," the doctor said calmly.

49

"That's right," said I, "give them tests!"

"We'll *all* take tests," he said again, and this time I heard him.

Well, I agreed; it was the sporting thing to do. After all I used to taste their cod liver oil first to show them that it wasn't so bad, and the least I could do was go along with the gag here.

Personality tests are very uncooperative things. They won't give an inch. Nothing is ever grey. It's either black or white, and no nonsense. They don't let you quibble or qualify your answers, and if there's one thing I like to do, it's qualify my answers. "Well *yes*, I *suppose*, but not *always*—it depends upon—" and my voice goes up to a whine or down to deceptive softness, depending upon how I feel. So I whined and complained (to myself) all through the test because it was so unfair to me, but I doggedly finished it, naturally painting as rosy a picture of myself as possible.

"Come back Thursday," said the good doctor as he collected our tests. I watched him as he tucked them away in his desk. There went my lovely personality in the drawer, and we'd soon *see* what the problem was and get it all squared away.

We went back Thursday. The doctor had our personalities all laid out on graphs. You haven't lived until you've seen your Christian personality all laid out on a graph.

"Son number one," he said, "he's okay."

"Oh?" I said.

"And son number two," he said, "he's okay." And then,

"Mrs. Barrett, when can *you* come back?"

I went back. And I found out *who* wasn't getting along with *whom,* and who the culprit was.

Me.

I found it out in the shortest possible order, too. Not because I was spiritual but because it was costing me money and I was not about to fool around.

When you differ from others, take five minutes to honestly try to see it from *their* point of view, *their* background, *their* personality. And stop to think that if you had their genes and chromosomes, their parents and grandparents with their backgrounds, right or wrong, you would see the thing exactly as they do. There are some cultures where wine is accepted as a matter of course. And some cultures where many wives are permissible. And some cultures where it is all right to eat people. It may not be *right,* but it's *so.* And if you were born there, that's the way *you* would look at it. This is extreme, to be sure, but the same rule of thumb applies in lesser things.

About criticism. In any discourse on personality, we are admonished to learn to take criticism. Indeed, no book would be complete without it. J. B. Priestley said, "We live in an age when no man of any importance ever admits he is wrong." Sometimes we think it *is* too bad we have to take criticism at all, for it is just another of those dreadful gnats that plague us and spoil all our plans for doing as we please. But in our more thoughtful moods we realize that people who are surrounded by "yes" men may not have the best of it after all; indeed they are tragic figures. They go on their way, with no one ever daring to cross them, and they manage to do everything but grow. In any case, as long as we give it we may as well be resigned to taking it also. The question is, how to swallow this draught as painlessly as possible?

There are two schools of thought on the subject. One is to consider the source. It is said of President Lincoln that one of his aides went to him once and reported that Mr. Seward had questioned his judgment on a certain matter; indeed, that Mr. Seward had said that the President was a fool. Mr. Lincoln walked over to a window and gazed thoughtfully out for a few moments, and then turned and said, "Mr. Seward is a very astute man. If he thinks I am a fool, then I must be a fool."

That would seem to be the end of it, with nothing more to be said. But it is just too pat. There is a trap. For the truth is, we are not all as noble and discerning as Mr. Lincoln, and it is just too easy for us to say "I have considered the source. I have given it mature deliberation. And I've concluded that the person is an idiot and has no idea what he is talking about." We are too prone to "consider the source" and conveniently ignore it if it is, in our opinion, not worthy of our consideration.

The other school of thought is to "consider the criticism for itself."

That's a harder rule to swallow, but a more profitable one, if you are serious about the matter of being honest with yourself. For the truth is that sound criticism may come from a very poor source, a very poor source indeed. Some of the soundest criticism we may receive may come from an ugly source and be vitriolic and humiliating, leaving us figuratively raw and bleeding so that the very covers on our bed hurt our flesh when we get home to lick our wounds. It *is* possible to be so hurt that it seems almost physical; indeed this phenomenon has a sound medical basis. Our emotions do affect our bodies, and the phrase "I was sick with humiliation" is all too true. At such times, to crawl off by yourself and coldly excise the criticism with the precision of a surgeon, and put it figuratively in a bottle, away and apart from its source, and from your smarting feelings, and dissect it, is no mean feat. It can excoriate. It can hurt beyond words. But if you do it in the light of the Holy Spirit (not a two-way conversation, but an honest desire to know the truth and a willingness to listen) it could conceivably change your life. But do it without morbid introspection, without flagellating yourself with every little criticism that comes your way. Here is the criticism. Is it valid? Forget who *said* it. The most important rule in this whole business is to *forget who said it*. Take it to God. If it's valid, act upon it; if it is not, forget it.

People react adversely to criticism in various ways, and the reactions come in many guises, but they all seem to fall into three categories.

There is the *superior* way. This is a hard one to cope with. It leaves the critic totally helpless and hamstrung, and if the one criticized is volunteer labor there is trouble afoot. Mr. A (who is in authority and only doing his duty) goes to Mr. B with criticism that is valid, constructive, couched in diplomatic terms and voiced in cheerful good will.

And Mr. B draws himself up to his full height and says, "Well! If you don't like the way I've been doing it (and I must say I've been doing it this way for four years and nobody has complained) I shall be happy to move out and you can get somebody else."

And Mr. B has Mr. A there, for they both know that Mr. A can't get somebody else, and so there they are—stalemate.

Then there is the *inferior* way. A poor unsuspecting Sunday School superintendent approaches a teacher and offers a suggestion. It is valid, constructive, and his approach is in good taste. But to his consternation she begins to get teary. "Well," she says, and "Ohhhh—" furtively dabbing at her eyes. "If you don't like the way I've been doing it—" more dabbing, "Lord knows I've tried—I *know* I'm not capable but I'm doing my best—" more dabbing, "but if I haven't been doing it right, you can get somebody else and I'll gladly step aside—though I've been doing it this way for years and nobody has complained—" She looks at him beseechingly—"until now"—more dabbing—"but I'll gladly step aside—" And what can the poor chap do but get out his handkerchief and help her dab?

Don't be misled. She is issuing the very same ultimatum. In her very weakness is a terrible kind of strength; she is about as weak as a brand-new steel trap and about as helpless as a cobra. What she is saying, in fact, is that she intends to go right on doing things *her* way and if he does not like it he can get somebody else and she knows and he knows that he can't.

The *third* way is the most devious way of all. The one criticized faces his critic with a wide-eyed stare and answers too glibly, "I know. I *know*. I'm so glad you mentioned this. I've realized it for a long time. Put me on your prayer list." And the critic goes away all aglow thinking he has made his point, and never noticing that the stare was slightly out-of-focus, the remark did not mean a thing and the one criticized had no idea of changing at all. Sometimes it takes months to catch up with the culprit.

These examples are extreme and too pat, of course. Things are never quite this simple. Actually we react to criticism in various combinations of these three ways, consciously or unconsciously.

Of course we don't have to learn to *give* criticism; it is a talent we are born with. We practice it on our brothers and sisters as children—"I wouldn't be in the same family with a nut like you if I could help it!" (And I wouldn't be familiar with this illustration if I hadn't said it.) By the time we are adults we have it developed to a fare-thee-well, so that in any questionnaire concerning why people don't like other people (men don't like women, women don't like men, employees don't like employers, children don't like parents, etc.)—one of the most frequent answers is "He (or she) is too critical."

Why do we do it? Psychologists tell us that we all need to feel important, one way or another. One way to do it is to excel; another way to do it is to tear down someone else who excels. But this seems too pat. For each of us excels in something and we still go about picking at others. It does not matter what they do right—we find something they do wrong, and zero in on that.

It happens in the nicest places. Right in the church. And with the nicest people. I remember a man-and-wife teaching team once, in an adult department. The wife had a genius for organization and detail; she was the epitome of efficiency. The husband seemed singularly unqualified for the job. He was inept, bungling, totally disorganized and inefficient and forgetful of details.

She criticized him, tore him down, carped at him and complained about him to anyone who would listen. Everything she said about him was true. Except for one little point she overlooked.

Everybody loved him.

If only she had recognized his genius for friendship and rejoiced that they *complemented* each other; if only she had kept her mouth closed, quietly done the organizing and let him be lovable which was his greatest talent. What a class that would have been!

If you *have* to criticize, do it in love and in fear and trembling; if you have any doubt that it is necessary, don't.

Don't wait to be discovered. When gold was discovered in Alaska, people from everywhere went rushing to the spot. "There's gold in them hills!" was an irresistible invitation to go find it. People braved unbelievable hardships and dared death itself to get it.

But the awful truth is, if there is "gold" in you nobody is going to take such risks. We rush through this busy life in this modern day as if we were driving like mad on a six-lane highway and other people rush past us with a roar and nobody is going to stop to find out what makes us so valuable.

To borrow the sentiments from the immortal poem—"I love you for reaching into my heaped-up heart and passing over all the foolish things you must have seen there, and having the patience to dig until you found all the lovely things that were there all the time, just waiting to be discovered...." It's a beautiful thought. But unfortunately it just isn't realistic. In point of fact, nobody is going to have time to lift up the hood of your personality like the hood of your car and clean away the sludge and tighten the loose bolts and connect just the right things that will make you spark. If you are going to spark, you are going to spark on your own.

No one is going to lift the hood of your personality like the hood of your car and tighten up the loose bolts.

So don't be the sort of person who has to be explained. "I know he seems taciturn and choleric and he looks as if he might bite your head off—but really, when you get to *know* him, he's a darling!" Well, are you now? Then why don't you show it? People don't have time to go digging, and the chances are you'll go to your grave leaving a trail of broken hearts and hurt feelings behind you without anyone's ever finding out just what a darling you were.

Or the sort of a person who has to explain himself. "The reason why I am so aggressive and offensive and obnoxious—and my dear you will never believe this—is because I really have an inferiority complex, and I'm compensating!"

You are compensating? So is everyone else, for one reason or another, and no one else is going to take time to find out why you are compensating or for what. All they can see is the surface, and the surface is that you are aggressive and offensive and obnoxious.

Or the sort of a person who lives in a vacuum, with no particular commitment to anything, the kind of whom is said "He opened the door and nobody came in."

I read this in a novel about school teachers once: "He was a rather vacuous person with nothing in particular right or wrong about him except that he seemed to dislike the curriculum and had no interest that I could see in the kids." What a horrible indictment.

Or the sort of person who takes his problem-riddled disposition as a matter of course, blaming it on the fates. There was a comic strip in which two dogs were talking. The little beagle said to the big bull dog, "Herbert, why are you so mean and nasty?" "Oh," said Herbert, looking hopelessly forlorn, "it all started when I was a little pup." He heaved a heavy sigh. "Nobody loved me." The beagle looked aghast. "*No*body?" he said sympathetically. "Why?" And the bull dog suddenly bared his teeth. "I was too mean and nasty," he said with relish.

Can this be I?

"How do you do?"

The Greeks had a word for it: "Act Successfully." And the Romans: "How is your strength?" And the French: "How do you carry yourself?" And the Germans: "How do you find yourself?"

It's a good question.

More often than not we don't like to come rignt out and say.

One wag reports a conversation between a doctor and his very despondent first-time patient.

"Do you like your job?"

"Yes."

"Like your boss?"

"Yes."

"Do you have any hobbies?"

61

"Yes."

"Enjoy them?"

"Yes."

"Friends?"

"Yes."

"Enjoy them?"

"Yes."

"Are you married?"

Sometimes we don't really know, until somebody draws it out of us.

Thomas Huxley the English psychologist jumped in a cab once and shouted to the driver, "Drive fast!" After a block he said, "Do you know where you're going?" "No," said the driver, "but I'm driving fast!"

I had a little friend once, a high school girl who came to my cabin at a summer conference to talk. Her problems were legion and she wasn't getting along with anybody, least of all herself. We talked at length, then and many times afterward, over a period of two or three years. Then I lost track of her.

And then a few years later, she suddenly appeared on my doorstep, looking very much the same—a sort of fresh-scrubbed kid, enormously intelligent—her IQ undoubtedly exceeded mine by an embarrassing margin—with huge pathetically lonely eyes pleading through her flip manner. We went out by the pool and she took off her sandals and dangled her feet in the water and talked and talked as if we'd never been separated. Her circumstances were different but the dreary tale was the same. She wasn't getting along with anybody, and again, least of all, herself. She had married, and had had a baby. But she had left her husband, gotten a job, and was living alone in an apartment; the baby had been with her mother for several months. This was her day off and she'd been just driving around for hours, with nothing to do, and she was bored.

"Nothing to do?" I asked. "Why didn't you see your baby on your day off?"

"Oh he doesn't know me any more," she tossed it off lightly. "He's so used to my mother now, he doesn't even know I'm alive."

I was too nonplused for the moment to scare up an answer. It would have been easy to give her advice, to scold her, but the years had taught me the futility of that. Before I could reply she said, "D'you know what I really want to do? I want to give up my apartment and go live with my girl friend."

"And what does your girl friend do?"

"She's a beautician." And then after a slight hesitation, "Well she *is* one, but she's not working just now. Actually—well actually she's lost her job. She's an alcoholic and I thought—if I could go live with her I might be able to straighten her out."

Monstrous? Yes. She had been talked to, ostensibly led to the Lord, prayed over, helped, worried over and had had psychiatric help. But she had built an insurmountable wall between herself and

63

people and between herself and God. Her circumstances were different but her tale was the same dreary one; she wasn't getting along with anyone including herself, and her confusion was legion.

I took her inside, gave her some tea, talked with her and prayed with her again, but I sent her away as confused as when she had come. She had listened to me without hearing. I asked her to come back, but she disappeared and for all I know she is still as confused about herself, and still trying to straighten other people out.

Though our sins and faults may be less flagrant, too often our story is the same; we dash through life oblivious to our own shortcomings, trying to straighten other people out.

I was at a luncheon-fashion show once. The models were wafting in like perfume, filling the room with beauty and glamour, dressed in "look-but-don't-touch" outfits, beyond both my pocketbook and figure. I was a most unlikely candi-

date for a customer on both counts—I'd gone primarily to the luncheon, and the fashion show was incidental. But one svelte model, size 6, drifted up to us dressed in a stunning beige suit. And one outsized lady leaned forward and whispered coyly, "Do you have this in size 44?"

We honestly don't *know* the answer to "How is your strength?" and "How do you carry yourself?" and "How do you find yourself?"

And in some areas we never do find ourselves at all.

Psychologists tell us to "know ourselves," to "adjust to ourselves," to "accept ourselves," and to "forgive ourselves." These are the basics, they say, and we cry back "What rot!" and "I cannot understand why Christians need psychology," and "if we are really spiritual we are above such things," and "these are man-made rules."

And so we throw psychology out. All of it.

Which seems to me, to use an old bromide, like throwing the baby out with the bath.

We may not be able to "know ourselves" or "adjust to ourselves" or "accept ourselves" or "forgive ourselves" and make a go of it, humanly speaking, but we *can* know ourselves and adjust to ourselves with the enlightenment of the Holy Spirit, and accept ourselves because God has accepted us, and forgive ourselves because he has forgiven us. To refuse to accept ourselves and forgive ourselves, and to flagellate ourselves for our past sins, after he has told us plainly that, in Christ, we *are* accepted and forgiven, is to fly in the face of his word.

For although these basic principles do not and

cannot work, outside of God, they can and do work when we add the enlightenment and power of the Holy Spirit of God in our lives.

To throw them out is like refusing to accept vitamin therapy just because vitamin pills weren't mentioned in the Bible.

To consider them and apply them, knowing that they are not the whole answer, but that they go a long way toward helping us to be honest with ourselves, is to apply practically what God has already told us. And if we know these principles, he has more to work with in dealing with us.

It is not the purpose of this book to deal with these principles per se, but there are some very simple questions we might ask about ourselves. Honest answers might prove to be life-changers.

They are simple but they are not easy. For we have such a penchant for calling one thing another. I brought up two boys alone and people would come up and say "you poor dear brave darling," and I'd say, "Yes," with a gallant little sigh, "but the Lord is with me." Actually I was having the time of

Yes, . . . but the Lord is with me...

my life; I would not have swapped my woe for anything. If any one had accused me of self-pity I'd have picked up my halo and gone home. But self-pity it was, nonetheless, and the truth did not come out for many years. When it did, after I got over the shock, I learned to laugh at it. I still have this proclivity but now I know the culprit for what it is.

Can you face your physical limitations? You have high blood pressure and the doctor says you can't have salt, you can't have pepper, you can't have coffee—and he names all the things you can't have. And you know the old saw about the doctor who said all these things to his patient and added, "If you don't obey these rules you will die." And the patient said, "If I do obey them I might as well die; there'll be nothing to live for."

There's the man who died of a heart attack. Everyone was surprised and shocked. But one of his friends said, "I walked with him on a mountain trail, a year ago. He had to stop and rest. I asked him what was the matter and he said he had pains in his chest and he was short of breath. I asked him why he did not go to a doctor. He answered that he did not because he knew what the doctor would say: that he would have to give up coffee and he would have to give up smoking and he would have to give up climbing mountain trails. And he was not about to." He was not willing to face his physical limitations, and chose to die instead.

Most of us have no difficulty in facing our physical limitations. We know how much we can do, and when we're headed for a breakdown somewhere in our bodies, we take medication or rest or do whatever needs doing, for the law of self-preservation is strong. Some of us do not. We go on, driving ourselves, thinking perhaps that we'll be the exception to the rule, or thinking perhaps that we are being noble, or thinking perhaps that we are being spiritual; it is difficult to say. What motivates us is between ourselves and God, and not for the rest of us to analyze or criticize.

But, generally speaking, facing our physical limitations is the easiest thing we do. The other limitations are not so easy.

Can you face your mental limitations? An engineer might walk into a new job. He has to face the fact that he is an engineer, he is not a writer. So he gets some one else to write his copy for him. He is a very smart engineer.

You walk into a new department in a Christian organization or in a church. The smartest thing you can do is recognize your mental limitations and realize that there is plenty of talent for you to draw on; you cannot do it all yourself. One of the saddest churches I know was one in which a misguided soul with more zeal than talent had not accepted his limitations. He'd lost his chiefs and he'd lost his Indians and everything was falling apart because he insisted upon doing everything himself; he had never learned to delegate authority because he thought he could do everything.

I walked into a Sunday School situation once as Christian Education director. And I, being both a coward and very lazy by nature, and therefore being absolutely agreeable to recognizing my limitations, promptly sleuthed out all the talent available.

It was there, in abundance.

There was the woman who was head of the art department in the high school: she took charge of our craft and supervised it and ordered all our craft supplies. And a woman who delighted in being social and had a talent for that sort of thing: she lined up couples to serve snacks on Sunday nights for the young people. And a woman who was the dietician of the local high school: she ordered paper plates and cups and food and planned our snacks a year ahead with great efficiency and know-how. And a woman who just delighted in helping, one way or another: she lined up cars for transportation to VBS or choir practice or whatever—just got the kids in when they could not get there by themselves. And a man who was head of the music for all the city schools: he made madrigals and choruses and choirs a delight to the young people.

We had well-supervised craft, good snacks planned a year ahead, good transportation for those who would never have come in otherwise, good music—and fun. And we had a growing vital alive Sunday School we never would have had if I'd tried to do it all by myself. And I found these people right within our own church membership.

The result? After I left, it was six months before anyone noticed. They said, "She's *gone?* When'd she go?"

Yes, most of all, we'd had good lay leadership. Not only in the things mentioned, but in teachers, in superintendents, in sponsors of evening groups, in leaders too numerous to mention. Because I scouted people out, ferreted them from their hiding places, cajoled them into doing what they'd never thought of doing before, told them they had a talent for doing what I could not do myself.

And me? I confined myself to the few things *I* could do; if I'd ever got turned loose on crafts or music or snacks or any of the rest of it, that church would have staggered under the resultant chaos for years. I knew my mental limitations.

Can you face your emotional limitations? Or do you plunge headlong into relationships and situations knowing that disappointment is imminent?

It is true, in the main course of events, when we are in the will of God, both relationships and situations might disappoint us, and if we are in the will of God we shall have his grace to prevail. But so often we dash off on side-paths, and I have a sneaking suspicion that we have a perverse desire to *be* disappointed; it is a neat way of blaming our gloomy outlook on life on some one or something else.

"I knew before I trusted him that he was going to let me down." But you did, and sure enough, he did let you down.

"I knew when she made that promise she had no intention of keeping it." But you relied on it, and, sure enough, she did not keep it.

"I knew when he flattered me and told me he loved me, he did not mean it." But you believed him, and, sure enough, he did not mean it.

"I saw the end of this experience before I began it, that it would end disastrously." But you began it and, sure enough, it did end disastrously.

And so we go off wailing at people's cruelty and

70

deceit when all the time the red flags were waving. And now we have fodder to feed upon for years to come, and a neat excuse for being gloomy.

So much for the side-paths. Back to the will of God.

Even in the will of God there are all sorts of little things that can trip us up in facing our emotional limitations. Our first great problem is that we don't realize we have them.

We know we have financial limitations. We learn this early. Who of us does not remember going to the candy store with our first penny? I remember it well. In my case it was Mr. Flannigan who patiently slid the glass doors back and forth and pointed and said, "This one?"

"No, that one."

"This one?"

"Yes. No, I think, *that* one."

And I would take up ten agonizing minutes of that poor man's time to choose what I wanted. The first time I embarked upon this exciting adventure, I put my hand way up high to take my purchase and made a great discovery. It seemed he wanted my penny before I could have my candy. What a dreary business. How complicated life was turning out to be. Why couldn't I have my candy and keep my penny, too? It seemed that if I wanted something I had to spend something, namely, my penny.

And as life went on I learned that money was limited. I could not pretend there was more when there wasn't. Whenever I did—(and I did)—the unpaid bill reminders soon straightened me out.

Our emotional energy has the same limitations.

71

But for some unfathomable reason we throw it around as though there were no end to it. There *is* an end to it. We are endowed with just so much and when it is gone we are depleted, we wake up in the morning exhausted, we are depressed. And we remain this way until we straighten out and replenish the supply.

The problem with emotional energy is that we are spending it anyhow whether we want to or not; the trick is to spend it on the right things and not dribble it away on things that do not further our progress.

We dribble it away on useless daydreaming. I used to imagine that there were mountains of ice cream in my backyard and I could just walk through the foothills and shovel it in. I don't know why I did not add nuts and chocolate syrup as long as I was at it but my imagination was limited. My favorite daydream was that I would be enabled to see answers above the teacher's head that were invisible to everyone else. That was a corker and far exceeded all my other daydreams, for it was obvious that if I were going to be able to see all the answers nobody else could see, life was going to be a snap.

On the other hand Neiman-Marcus, the great department store, was built on a daydream that *went* somewhere. I had lunch there with a native Texan who told me the story. Many years ago a nine-year-old boy worked in the stock room. And during lunch hour he would rush through his paper-sack lunch and then climb up on a box and make a speech about his dream of the most wonderful department store in the whole United States, much to the amusement of his colleagues. While I was listening to the tale I was watching a fashion show in the beautiful Neiman-Marcus dining room so I am a bit fuzzy on whether he was Neiman or Marcus but he was one or the other and he was not dribbling.

The crux of daydreaming is that it has to be realistic, and if it is, you must go ahead and carry out your plans. And the thing to remember about plans is that they must not degenerate back into daydreaming.

You can daydream for the rest of your life but it exacts a toll and that toll comes out of your store of emotional energy.

We dribble it away on griping. Industry knows that griping takes up an unbelievable amount of energy. GI's are notorious gripers; they're not allowed to do any thinking for themselves and griping is the only outlet many of them have. Son number two wrote me from Germany for three years, griping about the army and the weather and the food and the natives and an assortment of other things and finally when his hitch was up he wrote me a letter with the usual amount of gripes and ended it with, "PS: I've re-enlisted." Then he went to Vietnam and he had no more time to gripe; he kept sending home purple hearts. When the really big issues are at stake and we are busy getting bullets and shrapnel dug out and death is battering at our doors, griping about the ordinary annoyances of life seems a bit foolish.

We dribble it away "underground." A fancy

term for this is "suppressed emotions." And no wonder we are prone to this one. We are not supposed to show our emotions. Except when we are in love. Then we lose our appetite and start bumping into hydrants and everyone says, "He's in love. Isn't it beautiful?" But even there a few cynics will think us a bit silly.

We start bumping into hydrants and everybody says, "He's in love. Isn't it beautiful?"

Why can't a man cry? He isn't supposed to; it is not in our culture. To cry is to be a sissy. Though men are singularly shortchanged in this area, we are *all* shortchanged in almost every other area. We are not allowed to show our emotions; it isn't well-bred.

But our emotions are going to reach out somewhere. They are going to be spread around inside doing all sorts of mischief—(we might wind up with something nice and polite like high blood pressure or ulcers; we might really splurge and go off and have a nervous breakdown)—or they are going to be utilized for the good.

The thing to do is to steer our emotional energy

into areas where it is going to do the most good.

Do you hate to travel? The waiting, the weather, the delayed planes, the cancellation of flights, the loneliness of hotel rooms, the absence of the family and familiar surroundings, the inconvenience of it all.

Now if you are traveling for pleasure it is an entirely different matter; you take all these inconveniences in your stride for the pure joy of going where you want to go and seeing what you want to see. You got to Lake Galilee and the luggage was not aboard? You had to wait for hours before you could even get your toothbrush? No matter. There's Lake Galilee and all its beauty with the fishing boats, just as you'd imagined, and you forgot about the luggage and went on to enjoy Lake Galilee. It matters not, the inconvenience.

But do you *have* to travel just to get there, and all these things pall on you? I did. And they palled on me. The dirt, the living out of a suitcase, the delays, the weather, all the rest of it. I just wasn't emotionally equipped for it. I'd rather have been home with my feet in the oven. I was and am incurably lazy, and an incurable homebody. But did I give up traveling? I did not. I decided to write a book. I wrote on planes, in waiting rooms, in hotel rooms, wherever, and got so absorbed in the book that I did not even realize that I was going through all this discomfort. I avoided the thing about traveling that bothered me. The book turned out to be "Storytelling—It's Easy", but the thing that mattered was that it kept me so absorbed that I was transported to a new world where there was no time to even think about discomfort or to fret. And during the last few agonizing chapters, in a small town in New Mexico where I was holed up for a week, I got acquainted with one of the elevator boys and it turned out that he was working just temporarily there; he really was a musician in a band and had to stop there because his mother was very ill and he had to go see her in the local hospital and pay her bills. We got so well acquainted that I'd punch the elevator button during the hours I knew he was on duty, and meet him by the elevator door and hand him a bunch of pencils, which he'd take downstairs and sharpen for me. He began to feel that we were collaborating on the book and we had many writers' conferences during my elevator trips to and from the dining room. Which led, quite naturally, to talks about the Lord.

If you have to travel and hate to, knit a sweater, read that book you've been meaning to get to, write some letters, do *something* to avoid the thing that irritates you.

Do you feel tied down at home? Do some exercises and get yourself in great shape, go on a diet (you have no idea how absorbed you can become), take a course in something, read, listen, try to understand others, write out your frustrations and tear them up, write out the marvelous and revealing sayings of the very children who are tying you down, look upon it as an adventure in learning and if you do you will learn, and there will even be laughs along the way.

Are you tied down with a mate, and it is no laughing matter? Stop asking the Lord to straighten *him* out; make a list of the ways you can avoid situations in your relationship that tax you beyond your emotional limitations.

You can't have children? Taking orphans home for weekends, having a Sunday School class, visiting hospital children's wards, can give you more children than you'll have time for. You can't have marriage? All the more time for a career or a calling.

Don't keep plunging head-on into people and situations that you are not emotionally equipped to deal with, and then go whining into eternity because this person or that situation was your undoing. There are too many things you can do to avoid the trouble or at least mitigate it.

Can you be flexible? I was speaking at an Executive Club dinner meeting once when flexibility stopped being a theory and became a hard fact. We were laughing and in the gayest of moods and I was exhilarated and happy at having such a wonderful audience—when suddenly at a table directly in front of me, an enormous man turned very very blue, and slumped over onto his plate. I stopped horrified. But people were still laughing. "There's a man here who is very ill!" I shouted, but they laughed harder than ever. "Please!" I was frantic by now. "I am serious. This man is very ill. Is there a doctor here?" It seemed an interminable time before they shifted gears and realized what was going on. Then three doctors sprang into action at once. They struggled through the crowd, trying to work their way past all the pushed-back chairs and the hotel ballroom suddenly seemed as large as a city block as we waited what seemed forever before they reached the stricken man. They put his arms over their shoulders and carried him off, still in his chair. He was unconscious. There was a dead silence. We watched them struggle through as people made room. Then they disappeared through one of the back doors of the ballroom. And we were alone with each other, the audience and I. Obviously I could not go on with the previous nonsense. So I switched to a poignant anecdote about Fanny Crosby, during which I fervently hoped the program chairman would get up and call the whole thing off. Just as I was finishing it, two of the doctors reappeared in the rear doorway. I stopped again. "I know you are all as deeply concerned as I am," I said, "Two of the doctors have come back and I am going to ask these gentlemen to tell us about our friend." And they called out that the man was all right, on his way to the hospital, and apparently suffering from nothing more than acute indigestion. (I never found out whether the third doctor went to the hospital with the victim or used the mishap as an excuse to get away from my speech.)

We all sighed a great collective sigh, as one person. Then a man in the rear of the ballroom jumped up and shouted "If you don't finish that story you started before, I'll die!" The applause and laughter were outrageously explosive, but they were born of relief.

I leapt into the unfinished story with great glee and we were well on our way to identifying with it again—when suddenly a woman at the speakers' table jumped to her feet and went sobbing to the nearest exit. This was the moment when I considered the idea that my running, fleet of foot, for another exit might be the next sensible flexible thing I could do. Only the fact that the program chairman gave me a sign to go on with my speech prevented me. This, and the fact that my shoes were off and kicked out of reach under the speakers' table.

I learned later that the sobbing woman's husband had slumped in the same manner, in that same ballroom, practically in that same spot, a year previous. But he had died of a heart attack.

We had run the gamut of emotions from A to at least K and the thing that saved the evening was that we were all *flexible*.

D. L. Moody was flexible. He could not stand to be tied to a rigid program. In the midst of his message, if he felt that the audience was restless (it is difficult to imagine that any of his audiences could be restless) he would stop and ask Mr. Sanky to sing a song. It was the same way in his life. (This is not to say that every time something went wrong in his life he asked Mr. Sanky to sing a song.) But in reading six of his biographies I discovered that, though he had a single eye for God, when the various and sundry frustrations and interruptions and disappointments came along, he was absolutely flexible. He took what came with good humor and circumvented it, found another way, got the job done somehow; if it would not work *this* way it would work *another* way, and let's not stop and sulk or quibble about it.

79

How many Sunday Schools are dying on the vine because those in authority are not flexible? "But we've always done it this way," they cry and the fact that it has never worked is quite lost in the din.

I received a Christmas note from a dear friend in Loudenville, New York a week ago, and she said, "I had surgery for cancer on my birthday. How's that for a new idea in a birthday present? A few years ago when all signs pointed to cancer I was so scared I got converted; there are all sorts of ways to come to Christ, aren't there? But when I found I *did* have it I was as serene, and am as serene, as the beautiful Christmas story."

Now this kind of flexibility is straight from God and leaves me stunned with admiration. It is an extreme example, of course. But the point is, I have always found this woman flexible in little things in her life. And because she formed this habit of being flexible in little things she is able to weather this great storm. It is not the crisis it might have been if she had formed the habit of being *in*flexible so that it was worn into a deep groove and any change in her life or in her plans was absolutely unacceptable. It is true that her deep faith in God is unmovable. But it is also true that God has something to work with. He will not have to sidetrack and repeat and repeat; he will be able to go straight to her heart. I don't know what they are working out together. But from her words, "I am as serene as the beautiful Christmas story" I suspect that it will be something very wonderful.

It is only when we form the habit of being flexible in all the little things that we can become flexible, at last, in the hands of God in the big things that come our way.

But to say "be flexible" without examining the obverse, is not quite fair. There are certain aspects of being "inflexible" that we cannot ignore. Let's look at the dictionary.

Inflexible: 1. not flexible; incapable of or resistant to being bent; rigid; *an inflexible rod.* 2. of an unyielding temper, purpose, will, etc; immovable: *He is a man with an inflexible will to succeed.* 3. not permitting change or variation: unalterable: *arbitrary and inflexible laws.* Syn. 1. unbendable, stiff. 2. rigorous, stern, unrelenting, unremitting, stubborn, obstinate, intractable, obdurate, unbending, adamant. INFLEXIBLE, RELENTLESS, IMPLACABLE, INEXORABLE imply having the quality of not being turned from a purpose. INFLEXIBLE means unbending, adhering undeviatingly to a set plan, purpose, or the like: *inflexible in interpretation of rules*: *an inflexible will.* RELENTLESS suggests so pitiless and unremitting a pursuit of purpose as to convey a sense of inevitableness: *as relentless as the passing of time.* IMPLACABLE means incapable of being placated or appeased: *implacable in wrath.* INEXORABLE and UNBENDING mean stern, rigorous, and unmoved by prayer or entreaty: *inexorable in demanding payment.* 3. undeviating.

There it is. All of it.

And if we are inflexible and want to keep it this way, we can justifiably cry, "Oh *ho!* I *am* inflexible, and what are you to say? I am inflexible in the gospel, and in keeping the rules; I am unalterable in my faith; I'll not be turned from my purpose for Christ."

Sounds good. And it is. We have a case. But let's not run it into the ground.

D. L. Moody was inflexible in these things. He never swerved from his purpose, not for a moment. But his son Willie tells us* that he was most flexible in his human relationships, and always willing and ready to admit it when he was wrong. He would go to his children's bedrooms at night and say, "Are you awake? I can't go to sleep till I talk to you. I'm sorry I lost my temper." Or, "I'm sorry I was so unreasonable. Will you forgive me? Christ would not have acted like that." And his hand on their foreheads was like the weight of a library dictionary, but all they felt was the weight of love. And Willie cried out in a passionate teen-age tribute: "Other kids tell me they cannot go to their dads and just talk and hope to be understood; they say they can't because their dads are 'always right' and they are 'always wrong.' They can't talk to their dads the way I can talk to you. I could always talk to you. You always understood. There was nothing I could not tell you."

He was inflexible in his purpose for Christ, but flexible in his dealings with human beings. He backed down when he was wrong. He knew his human failings.

Those of us who pride ourselves in being inflexible might well look into it. What are we being inflexible *about?*

*Pollock's Biography of Moody

Do you lose your temper? I threw my hand mirror out of my bedroom window once when I was away at school. I would have gotten away with it except that the window happened to be closed at

I would have gotten away with it except that the window happened to be closed at the time.

the time. I was called to the office and told that I had better learn to curb my temper or I would not be around there very long.

When I married I became very docile and do not recall ever losing it. (I sulked in martyr-like silence instead, which may be a bit sneaky but it makes you feel a lot more spiritual. One of the greatest blessings of marriage is that it gives you somebody else to blame things on.)

When I had the whip hand again and full responsibility and children dependent upon me, I found to my dismay that the temper I'd thought was dead, was only in the pit getting recharged and re-tired and re-gassed, ready to get out on the track and back into the race again.

In retrospect, the pattern is plain enough. I lost

my temper most easily when my security was threatened, and when I felt woefully inadequate or guilty or just plain frightened.

The degree of the explosion of your temper rarely has anything to do with the seriousness of the event that triggered it off. You can lose it equally with your children whether they dropped a course in school or did not hang up a coat. And the event that triggered it is not important. The important thing is what it did to some part of your personality. It hit you some place where it pinched.

Do you lose your temper with your children? Watch it; you may be projecting your own weaknesses into their behavior, seeing yourself in them.

Do you lose your temper with your mate? Watch it; there may be a sneaky feeling of guilt lurking somewhere.

Do you lose your temper with your co-workers and friends? Watch it; the culprit may be a projection of a deep sense of dissatisfaction with yourself.

And remember: whether you shout or throw a hand mirror through a window or speak in low measured tones of ice or vitriol, or simply turn purple and go off somewhere and listen to your ulcers drip, you are still losing your temper.

Are you selfish? Of course overt selfishness is so obvious that it would hardly pay to discourse on it at any great length here. If in your home and in your job and in your social contacts, it turns out that you are always the one who gets your way, then you are selfish and you jolly well know it.

One of the classic basic story-plots is the parent who slaves and sacrifices for his children and then plagues them all with gentle reminders of said sacrifices, keeping them from fleeing the nest, or, if they do, continuing to live their lives for them and strangling them in the end, as surely as if they had been strangled physically.

An equally classic story-plot is the parent who slaves and sacrifices for a child and then, when the child has gone on to fame and fortune, fades into the background and dies a lonely death.

These are two melodramatic extremes. Between them there are enough degrees of selfishness and unselfishness to stagger the imagination, some of them obvious, and some of them so subtle that we can coddle them all our lives without ever suspecting it.

Psychologists tell us that no one commits any act or does any deed unless the satisfaction he gets outweighs the pain. You give up a habit. It hurts to give up the habit. But the satisfaction of discipline gives you more pleasure than the habit did. If this be true, then the question is not "Are you selfish?" but "What kind of selfishness do you have?"

You will never know, without the light of the Holy Spirit. Selfishness goes to the very core of our Christianity.

Are you afraid to fail? Well it's no wonder. We are brought up in a culture that places an unrealistic emphasis on success. We are taught as children that it is a disgrace to fail. And we compound the error by passing on the same philosophy to *our* children.

Of course when we are cornered we say glibly that everybody makes mistakes and naturally we make mistakes like anybody else. But we don't believe it. Actually some of us secretly feel that we make more mistakes than anybody else. And some of us try to convince ourselves that we don't make any mistakes at all. The end result is the same. We are thrown by failure. We're afraid to be wrong.

What does this fear cost you? Is there a place in your church or your business that you will like to fill but you're afraid you will fail? Have you lost out in love and you're afraid to try a new relationship for fear you'll lose again? Did you make a speech and fall on your face and you're afraid to try again? Did you write a story and it was turned down and you're afraid to write another?

You don't need to take it lying down. Fail successfully. Take a sheet of paper and write it all down. Why did you fail? Why? Be honest. The answer might be so simple as to astound you. Step up on your failure as if it were a stepping-stone, and try again, leaving the mistakes out. Don't go through life practicing your mistakes.

If you break your arm, you get it set in a cast and nature deposits calcium around the break, and the chances are it will never break at that spot again; the calcium deposit has made the bone stronger there than it was in the first place. The mistake has been corrected. After a spinal fusion I asked the doctor if I'd always have to be careful of that spot. And he told me no, that I was so full of bone chips and nuts and bolts in that spot that though I might break my back in a dozen other places I was highly unlikely to break it *there.*

Failure can get you down only if you let it crush

you. You are going to fail again and again in different ways and in different degrees. Life is a succession of failures, most of them little ones. If it were not so we would never learn. Fail successfully. Thank God for the failure and for what it taught you and vow not to make that mistake again. But don't stop trying!

Tennyson's first manuscripts drew caustic criticism. Disraeli's first speech in the House of Commons was a dismal failure. Galileo was a laughingstock. Rudyard Kipling applied for a job as a reporter on a California paper and the editor not only turned him down but ridiculed his name in the process. E. Stanley Jones' mind went blank when he began his first sermon. He was about to give up when a girl giggled. That did it. The block was gone, and he's been preaching ever since.

But suppose you have failed in a relationship and you've gone over all the facts honestly, and you actually did not do anything wrong? This can happen. But even this kind of failure is not the end of everything. There may be a valuable lesson in it, a lesson God wanted you to learn. You may have been too dependent upon this other person for security, for entertainment, for counsel, for social poise, for strength, for *something* that was lacking in you. This person did not betray you or fail you or desert you—he *freed* you. (There are areas in my personality in which I never would have developed any strength if some dear friend hadn't booted me out.) Now you can stand there shivering with cold and despair and still be complaining about it bitterly years later, or you can fail successfully and develop in yourself the thing you were mooching from this person.

How many opportunities do you pass up, how many decisions do you not make, for fear you'll be wrong and fail? We don't marry, don't get better jobs, don't take that class, don't make that friend because we are afraid to try a new venture or we have tried it and failed and don't want to risk having a go at it again. We may say, "I didn't feel led to," and indeed we may be right. But more sins of omission have been committed under that guise than this world dreams of.

We have an obligation not to quit. A friend of mine told me about a play she had gone to, where the second act was a comedy of errors. The setting was a little cabin in a forest. A young couple came on the stage. The girl pointed to the cabin. "There it is!" she cried. But suddenly the little cabin went up into the air. "There it is," she said with some confusion, pointing upward. Then it came down again, hard, and billowed and swayed back and forth. She tried again. "There it is!" But it went up again. And came down. And so did the curtain. Within seconds the curtain billowed and fussed and the manager pawed his way out. "We're having a little confusion among our stagehands," he explained. "So if you will just be patient the cabin will be down to stay, we hope—" the rest of his discourse was drowned in laughter.

Did the audience go home? Did the management and the actors give up? No, they took their ups and downs in their stride, and went merrily on with the play.

**How confused
can you get?**

OUR TWENTY-TWENTY hindsight is terrific.

The Germans have a splendid noun for it: der Treppenwitz. Staircase wit. It is what the inarticulate man thinks of, after he has left the committee meeting or the party or the panel discussion or whatever, as he is walking down the staircase going home. It's his twenty-twenty hindsight.

You're confused? Take heart. So is everybody. Even the seers, the forecasters, the learned, the most gifted. Everybody.

I remember a radio program in Los Angeles where an internationally famous clairvoyant was scheduled for an interview to talk about his prowess in locating lost people, kidnapped children, stolen valuables and whatnot. But he didn't show up; he couldn't find the studio.

I was at a small social gathering once, and we got into one of those truth sessions. It did not start out to be one, but it did turn out to be one—it just "happened." I cannot remember what triggered it, but everybody began to tell what his problems were. Except me, of course. Naturally I did not have any problems; I had everything figured out. But *they* had problems, every one. And the problems were so diversified. No two people had the same one. One girl went on about how her whole life was a failure and it all hinged upon the fact that she had married. She was now divorced. She seemed to think that if only she had not married in the first place, everything would have turned out all right. Another girl was absolutely certain that all her problems stemmed from the fact that she had *not* married. Somebody else's problems hinged on the fact that he had doting parents. Another had problems because his parents had never paid any attention to him and had given him too much freedom. Another one's problem was his boss. And another's was her mother-in-law.

These various and sundry problems were completely diversified but they all had one common denominator. Not one of those people blamed his dilemma on himself. Every one of them was perfectly sure it had been caused by some other person or some set of circumstances beyond his control.

Because the evening had taken such a serious turn, we had a "word of prayer" before we broke up. Then everyone went home, as confused as he was before, taking his problem with him. For everyone's greatest problem was himself.

The secular world capitalizes on our confusion. It is appalling to realize that most of the merchandise that is sold, is sold by playing upon our subconscious. We are the victims of a multi-million dollar enterprise in depth probing, depth manipulation and symbol manipulation. The whole concept is enough to make us wrap up our accoutrements in a diaper and go back to Walden Pond armed with nothing more than a couple of safety pins and the bare necessities of life and start all over again, the mind pristine and uncomplicated.

People, according to this new and terrifying science, never buy a product, they buy a promise. A woman will pay a few cents for a cake of soap and several dollars for a jar of hormone cream. Why? The soap promises only to make her clean; the hormone cream promises to make her young.

Marketing research has, for some years, had us spotted as people of misty hidden yearnings and guilt complexes, given to impulsive acts, and prone to compulsive buying. They beam their messages to people of high anxiety, hostility, passiveness, aggressiveness and whatnot. Think of any trait you might have, consciously or unconsciously; they already have it computerized. They hit us over the head and get us to buy, to act, while we are "unconscious," as they put it.

They probe our everyday habits for hidden meanings and delve into the whys of our behaviour. They set up hidden cameras in super markets to record our eye blinks, on the premise that by the time we get up to the checking-out desk (if they have done their work well) we are in a trance, and the rate of eye blinks indicates how deep that trance is. (If the rate of your eye blinks is high you've gone over your budget.)

They can control our home lives, our social lives, our possessions, or children, our very attitudes, and custom-make us, like robots.

They do not want us to make purchases. Market research teaches that we are to be impelled to make what they call "splurchases."

And how do they compel us to buy? By appealing to our hidden needs. They appeal to our desire to reassure ourselves of our worth; (good luggage is a symbol of importance.) They appeal to our sense of power. When they advertise machinery they seldom show a long shot of the machinery; they show a big brawny and always ruggedly handsome man *operating* the machinery. We see his muscular arm pulling that lever and the implication is that he is just about to knock the stuffings out of a moun-

They show a big brawny and always ruggedly handsome man operating the machinery.

tain. They appeal to our ego-gratification. "This car will pull ahead and believe you us, you'll be *first* when the light turns green." They appeal to our snob appeal, and unfortunately they play havoc with us on this one. And they appeal to our desire to be creative. One cake-mix company realized this and put out their product so that we could add an *egg*. Pretty sneaky, that, but it worked.

They plan their packaging with meticulous care.

The package must have a dream-like quality. It is word tested—each word is carefully tested for hidden bloopers and bad word-association. And color! Women fall for red; men fall for blue. (It is not that women fall for red, but marketing realizes that most women are too vain to wear their glasses while shopping and red is the easiest color for them to see.) They don't care if we *like* the product; they just want us to *buy* it.

Advertising is resplendent with warm emotional overtones and promises of social status, overt or hidden.

The theory is carried over into planning office buildings; even there, prestige is played upon. Nothing is overlooked; every door slam has a personality. Nobody wants a teeny weak door slam any more. Or a hingy one. Or a squeaky one. A door slam should be important, compact, *big*. You simply must have an important door slam or you are not *in*.

To carry it to the ridiculous (and it already is) if you were building a new church, they would tell you to think big. Big impressive buildings, proper important door slams, big trees outside, big lawns. And while you're at it, if there are to be any dogs running over your lawns—*big* dogs, and no nonsense.

Even politica. candidates aren't elected any more; they're *sold* to the public. A politician puts himself in the hands of an agency right along with headache tablets and soap powder. And he doesn't run for election, he "goes on the market" just like merchandise. He sits meekly in a waiting room of an agency and waits for hours, hoping to be "taken on" if the agency is successful enough and has a reputation for "selling" political candidates. Market research takes him over to see what his inherent sales potential is and how great the task of engineering consumer desire might be. If he has something on the ball to begin with, then he has a high built-in demand potential. If he does not, then it must *be* built in. If he's been around for a long time, he's given the "new-improved" pitch. Like an old established product—(it's been around so long that if you try to rebuild its image you risk offending its old constituency, so the obvious thing to do is to shout that it's the same old thing, only new and improved). If he has nothing on the ball at all, market research might conclude that the problem is one of packaging; divert attention away from the contents; keep it on the package. And so they'll invent a new package.

One way or the other—a high built-in demand potential or a demand-potential the agency has built in, or the old established product now improved, or a bag of wind in a fancy package— they'll sell that candidate to you. And he is aware of this when he goes to that agency; otherwise he would not sit there so meekly and so long, to get sold. He's *merchandise*. And he jolly well knows it.

Actually he's a great deal less confused than we who elect him. One agency bragged about the successful marketing campaign it had done on one of our former presidents: "We sold him, just like toothpaste."

In the face of this multi-front assault on all our

senses and all our reason, it would seem easier to just give up, admit we're confused, and blunder it out as best we can. But let's not go down in defeat. There are a few simple rules we can put into practice that can lift us out of the doldrums and make life a great deal easier. We may not be able to master them all, but if we can master only one, we can be, like the song, "better than we are." Benjamin Franklin kept a "self-improvement" notebook, in which he laid down rules for himself. One of the most important rules was to stop being so dogmatic when he had to disagree with someone. He vowed to start his opinion with "I may be wrong, but—" And he stated in his autobiography that *following that one rule* revolutionized his relations with other people.

Now actually, this is a pretty smart thing to do. For if, in the end, you are proved wrong you can always say, "I *said* 'I may be wrong'—" so you are right even when you are wrong. You can't lose. And if you think this is a wishy-washy self-effacing way to go through life, remember that Benjamin Franklin did not go down in history as a milk-toast.

The biggest hurdle to get over is to accept the fact that you may not always be right. As highly unlikely as it may seem, it can happen, even to you. There are, however, a few basic rules in straight-thinking that can minimize this grim possibility.

Supplement the information you have with your own observations. We do this in small matters. Any "Wet Paint" sign will verify that we do. I was sitting in a car with a friend in a restaurant parking lot, late one afternoon, and we witnessed a little drama that would have been a natural for Candid Camera. A painter had just finished painting the side door. He hung a "Wet Paint" sign on the huge brass door-handle, and carried his paints over to his truck. As he walked away a group of people came along, hesitated at the door, then one of them opened it very carefully and let the others go in after which he touched the paint very gingerly before he went in himself. Almost immediately another group came along. By this time the painter was packing his truck and was watching grimly. This group went whole-hog. They all touched the paint. The painter went back and touched up the marks and started back to his truck, but even while he was doing so, another group was going through the same ridiculous pantomime. We watched for ten minutes while the little drama was repeated over and over again, with variations. One time the whole party got all the way in and the door closed.

And opened again.

And a hand reached out and touched that paint.

And a hand reached out and touched the paint!

Finally the painter saw us laughing, gave an exaggerated mock sign of resignation, climbed into his truck and drove off.

But the very people who would investigate a wet paint sign often accept enough misinformation, gossip, and prejudice to fill the average church with trouble enough to last for years.

We don't think straight because we jump to conclusions on inadequate information. You could say that a certain organization began as a small movement in an obscure part of the world, that it was despised, that its first leaders were hated, that it was limited almost entirely to the poor and the unlearned, and that it had no rewards or honors to confer. But there was more to the church than that.

A dossier could be given on a certain figure in history saying that he had an unhappy childhood, that his ambition to be an artist was opposed by his father, that he was self-educated, that he wrote a book that ranked in sales next to the Bible, that he emphasized and promoted the health of young people, that obstacles did not discourage him and that he was one of the most dynamic and persuasive speakers in history. But there was more to Hitler than that.

There may be one more fact. It's a pretty good guess that you can never get all the facts. And it's a pretty good idea, even after you've collected all the facts you possibly can, to still say, "So far as I know." There just might be one additional fact lurking somewhere to knock the props from under your conclusion.

Like the time when I was a child, an aunt I was visiting sent me to the store with a note. It was before I could read; that, and my own black heart, were my undoing. I handed the clerk the note and watched him fish a dozen foil-wrapped squares of candy out of a huge bowl and put them in a bag. He put my aunt's change in the bag too, handed it to me and like Mission-Pak, I was on my merry way. About halfway back to my aunt's the larcenous thought occurred to me; she would not miss one of those little candies, would she? To me twelve seemed like a whole bagful and because I couldn't read I just reasoned that she couldn't count. I grabbed at this temptation right off, lest I think about it too long and conquer it. I unwrapped a candy, popped the whole thing in my mouth and began to chew.

It was a bouillon cube.

Well it jolly well served me right.

When I got back to my aunt's I was still spewing bouillon and she decided I'd already been punished enough, physically. She did give me a good going-over verbally, though, and ended grimly: "Well you'll be cheap to feed anyhow. For the next few days when I want you to have bouillon I'll just give you a cup of hot water."

And the time I was standing around a counter in a ticket agency with a dozen or so other people, waiting for service. Suddenly I felt a sneeze coming on and I groped for my purse on the counter, opened it and fished wildly for a tissue. The woman standing next to me kept staring at me strangely, which did not surprise me for I know people do look a bit odd before they sneeze. I finally found the tissue, not where I thought I'd put it, and caught the sneeze just in time. She continued to stare. I looked at her with streaming eyes and smiled weakly while I finished mopping up. Just then my tickets were ready and when I stepped a bit to the side to reach for them my foot brushed—oh *no*. My own purse. It had been standing on the floor beside me. The purse I'd fished the tissue out of was hers.

And the time years ago when I was a Christian Ed. director, and I followed the junior highs down to the basement one Sunday morning to speak to them. We bumped our heads on the pipes overhead and groped our way through a narrow hallway and I thought, "What a dismal place to meet; this labyrinth of corridors and small rooms could all be made into one big beautiful bright room." So I drew some plans, I decorated it in my mind's eye all in subtle shades of green—I was even going to paint the piano green. I was all excited and enthusiastic about the project and I gathered all my facts. If you tore down this wall and this wall and *this* wall too—it could be done! I talked to my pastor and to a few key people about it, and finally faced the board with shining eyes. I had all my facts—but one. It turned out that if we tore down the walls, the first floor would fall in.

And the time I was dining with a friend in one of those restaurants where you stumble into what seems like a total darkness and you ask your escort to order for you because it is so feminine and dependent and besides it keeps him from knowing that you cannot read the menu without your glasses. We were groping our way along, following the headwaiter rather desperately lest he get too far ahead and we would lose him forever and never get out of the place again—when my friend spotted a woman whose beautiful blond mink stole had slid from the back of her chair and was in a heap on the floor. Gallantly he stooped to retrieve it. There was a low ominous snarl from the stole and my friend left the floor a foot beneath him. It was the woman's Seeing Eye dog. It was fur all right, but it was a fur that was still on a dog. There was one additional fact that my friend had not known about and it nearly bit his hand off.

Nothing is ever 100%. There is no life and no situation that is 100% anything, one way or the other. Everything is "up to a point." Nobody is ever 100% sane or insane, good or bad, efficient or inefficient, beautiful or ugly, intelligent or unintelligent, quick tempered or calm.

Is he a success? No matter how big a success he is, he's a success up to a point. Even Moses, the greatest patriarch who ever lived was a success up to a point. He struck the rock instead of speaking to it and never got into the promised land. And David, as successful as he was, remains a horrible example to beware when you think you stand, lest you fall.

Is he a failure? Not a hundred percent. Lincoln was a failure in everything he tried; in love, in business and especially politics. And he wound up being president.

Is he superior? Look at Einstein, one of the greatest brains the world has ever known. But he went to visit friends with a letter in his pocket, written by his wife, to be delivered to his hosts. It was a list of instructions to make sure he wore his sweater when he went out, took his pills, and in general, took care of himself. He was prodigiously superior in one area and absolutely childlike in other areas and had to be watched out for by his wife. Did he mind? Not a bit. He realized they counterbalanced each other and he leaned on her for some things and she leaned on him for others. He did not mind being totally inadequate in some areas; he knew he was smart enough in others.

Is he inferior? Not 100%. When Mathilde Wrede, the great missionary to the prisoners in Finland, went into a prison to visit a prisoner, he handed her an exquisitely carved ivory brooch. And she said, "I never saw anything so beautiful. Where did you get the ivory to carve it, my friend?" And he said, "It isn't ivory. It's an old soup bone. I laid it on the window sill to dry in the sun and the sun cleansed out all its impurities just as the Sun of Righteousness cleansed mine. And when all the impurities were gone I began my task. I have been months and months, carving it for you, because you told me about Jesus."

Things are not always what they seem. Don't say "This is the way it is," but rather, "It seems this way to *me*," and you'll be a lot closer to the truth. For we seldom see things as they are.

It would solve a lot of problems if we all had "instant replay," so that in any given situation where we are fuzzy about the details, we wouldn't go spouting off with one-sided opinions and hasty conclusions, only to find that our opinions left something to be desired and our conclusions were smudged with what we *thought* was the case.

People who watch live action football on TV

know about the instant replay. It gives them a second look. They see spectacular plays or crucial plays over again, to their delight or consternation, as the case may be. And they see controversial plays, not the way they thought they were, but the way they really happened: There is hardly a football fan who cannot remember some pass reception in some big game where an official called it a touchdown but the camera, particularly in slow motion on the instant replay showed clearly that the ball was caught outside the end zone. The fans booed it as they saw it. Or cheered it as they saw it. And the official called it as he saw it. But the instant replay had the last word.

In the game of life, we do not have instant replay; we see the thing only once. And we cannot go back and view it again—we have only our memory to serve us, and our memory is streaked with prejudices and wishful thinking and selfishness.

In saying "it seems this way to me" you are leaving yourself room to change, to reevaluate, to grow. And you are leaving yourself a handy loophole if it turns out you are wrong.

This principle is true in evaluating people, as well. "He's dull," we think. Well is he now? He may just seem dull to you. He may not be dull to someone else at all. And if you knew him better he may not seem dull to you anymore. We are all dull to some people in some areas.

If we could just learn to say "I may be wrong, but—" or "there may be one more fact," or "up to a point," or "it seems this way to me," the misunderstandings in our lives would be cut in half.

**Logic:
once over, lightly**

In this matter of logic, I run the gamut from illogical to irrational. I know the basic rules but have always been singularly inept at applying them.

Of course the peculiar logic of women is understood only by other women. I was driving along in a car with a man and his wife one time when the wife suddenly snapped the car radio on and quickly off again. "I thought it was on so I turned it on and it was off so I turned it off," she explained, which

I thought it was on so I turned it on, but it was off so I turned it off.

made her husband roll his eyes skyward but made perfect sense to me. Another time, during a week when Monday had been a holiday, I overheard a woman phoning, in the next office, and she said, "I should have called you sooner. But I thought Tuesday was Tuesday and Tuesday was Monday." And I knew exactly what she meant.

Men feel that these things are difficult to translate for they have already lost something in the original. But I feel that they are so whimsical in the original that it would be a shame to try to translate them. They might make more sense, but how very dull they would be.

We are told to think logically, which is a big order, for who of us can? We had no help in childhood. We were brought up on the facts that water runs downhill, that if you step on a crack you'll have bad luck, that you get warts from frogs, and that babies are found in cabbage patches.

And we do not get much help as adults. There certainly is a dearth of good examples. The overlapping of government functions defies all logic, in fact common sense. A public highway is under the jurisdiction of the Bureau of Public Roads of the Department of Agriculture. But if it runs through a park it is under the National Park Service of the Department of Interior. If it's in Alaska it is under the Engineer Corps of the War Department. Now that's a lot of bosses for one little road.

The Colonial Goat is under the Department of Interior if he lives in Hawaii and under the War Department if he lives in the Philippines and under the Navy Department if he lives in Guam.

If you shoot a fox in Alaska you must settle accounts with the Department of Commerce.

Bears really get mixed up. The Secretary of the Interior protects Grizzly Bears. The Secretary of Commerce protects Polar Bears. And the Secretary of Agriculture protects Brown Bears. And if a brown bear marries a black bear and they have twins and one is brown and one is black—

Yes.

The twins are under the auspices of two different federal departments.

Now the brain is a wonderful gadget but it has its limitations and with all these things militating against it, thinking logically is an uphill grind. We can never attain it, but one of the ways to come close to it is to spot *illogical* thinking. Here are some of the ways we misuse logic.

We overgeneralize. "Men are the best drivers," or "Women are the best drivers," or "Old people are the worst drivers," or "All nurses and school teachers are bossy," or "All women who do not wear makeup are spiritual," or "Doctors say that—" How much evidence? How big was the survey? Is this an educated guess or careless jumping to conclusions? And who doctors? People are people and there are always exceptions.

We get mixed up with cause and effect. I remember this well. Many years ago I drove to a church one night to speak, following directions as best I could, for there was a blizzard and visibility was zero-zero. Finally I found it and parked with great difficulty and went in. Nobody knew me. I encountered a young lady in a hallway and asked,

"Is the pastor here?" "Yes, he's around here some-place," she said, and hurried on. So did I. I entered a huge room where people of all sorts were rehears-ing for something. "Is the pastor around?" I asked with less aplomb than before. "No," they said, "we don't know where he is." I went on. Everyone I encountered reacted the same way so I decided to find the pastor's study. I wandered through a laby-rinth of corridors, feeling like the chap in search of the Minotaur of Crete and wishing I had a string tied to me so I could find my way out again. When I reached the pastor's study it was locked. I de-cided to go out into the sanctuary and sit in a front row and get discovered. I was just in time for the orchestra was beginning to play. Then the singing started. I caught the pastor's eye and he smiled, but did not indicate that I should go up on the plat-form. I thought all this very strange and was pon-dering on the cause of it all, when the song-leader-master-of-ceremonies spotted me and cried, "I see we have, of all people, Ethel Barrett here. I wonder if we could presume upon her to tell us a short story?" And everyone applauded with gusto. I went to the platform thinking this was a very odd way to get introduced, and told a short story. And sat down. We sang another hymn. And then—and *then*, the pastor got up and introduced the speaker of the evening who got up and proceeded to speak. I sat there in a state of shock. If I was the speaker of the evening; what was *he* doing here? And if he was here, what was I doing here? And if I did not belong here why did they ask me to tell a story? It was all very baffling and beyond my comprehension. I simply slunk out afterward, found my car and went home, all my logic askew.

The next morning I got a phone call from a pastor who wondered why I had not shown up at his church when all his plans indicated that I would and all his congregation had been waiting? The strange events of the night before fell into place. The cause was simple. I'd been in the wrong church. And the fact that the folk had recognized me and invited me to tell a story had compounded my error, which had been grievous enough to begin with. The proper church was on the same street, on an identical corner, five blocks down. I made amends, but that's another story.

Of course the law of cause and effect here is elementary. If you don't follow directions you will get in the wrong church.

We get personal. The other fellow is right (so everyone else thinks) but he is wrong (so we think) about something (it doesn't matter what). But instead of sticking to the issue, we say archly, "Of course he has a poor background," or "Did you know he went to one of those small colleges?" or "Of course everyone knows that he is henpecked to death at home and hasn't had an opinion in years," or "Did you know—" (with a look that indicates that you know plenty that no one else does) "—that he's divorced?" And we've "fogged up" the issue and discredited him on some other score. Now the poor chap is either right or wrong regardless of his background or personality or personal life. To fog up the issue and get personal is definitely out of bounds.

111

We appeal to authority. "I didn't like it. But the critics did. So it must be good." "Advertising has proved beyond a doubt that in this area we are most easily duped." "Scientific tests show—" "Four out of five doctors say—" "Fashion says—"

I tried to straighten my doctor out once on a certain subject and he thundered, "And what makes you think so?" "Well," I said, "you see I read this article—" Then he straightened *me* out. "And," he bellowed in conclusion, "we are sick of these articles in popular magazines, over simplifying and drawing pat conclusions—" He ended up with a stirring climax on how a little knowledge is a dangerous thing and then I left hurriedly, fearing for his high blood pressure.

But he had a point. And the point was one of logic. We appeal to "authority" and often it is merely popular opinion, or at best, the popularly *accepted* authority. Critics and fashion experts and magazine articles should not dictate to us.

We think in black or white. And there is no black

We think in black or white.

or white. Big issues are always grey. You can always make out a case for both sides. The truth lies somewhere in the middle. For example, some people think I am very very nice. Some people think I am a crashing bore. The truth lies somewhere in the middle.*

We use the false analogy. We choose one point to compare merits, and we invariably choose the point that serves our own cause. To de-twaddle this: here are two people of the same background and intelligence. One gets ahead in his profession; the other does not. And we cry "All people with background and intelligence should get ahead," ignoring the fact that the one who got ahead handled people better and was a better organizer.

Or we cry, "He's just like his father all over again." He is not like his father all over again. He's *him*. And he could not be exactly like his father any more than two snowflakes are alike. There might be an unknown factor in *this* situation that has not come to light yet.

To choose one point in which two people or two situations are alike and jump to the conclusion that they are therefore alike on all points is unperceiving, undiscerning, and incomprehensible. And besides it doesn't make sense.

Now these little warning signs of illogical thinking—overgeneralizing, muddying up cause and effect, getting personal, appealing to authority, thinking in black or white, and using the false analogy—are mere rudiments, to get you started.

*Actually I *am* very very nice, so this is a very poor example.

They never got me very far. For in the end I always get tripped up on two other elementary points.

"It goes without saying." This always stops me. When some one looks at me in a very superior manner and tosses off, "of course, it goes without saying, . . ." before he makes his point, he turns off my logic as surely as if he had flipped a switch. The implication is that if it goes without saying I should have known it all along. And I am so embarrassed that I didn't know, I climb out of the ring, all the ginger gone out of me.

"Any school boy knows" is the other one. I reason that if any school boy knows then I ought to know. So my logic flies out the window and I listen attentively hoping I'll soon find out; after all, I want to know what every school boy knows.

So I remain as I was. Running the gamut from illogical to irrational.

**Enthusiasm
is dynamite**

I READ IN AN IDAHO paper about an intrepid old warrior who had two outstanding traits; a boundless enthusiasm for life and a hearty disdain for failure; he absolutely did not know when to quit. Old Whitey was in his dotage but he was singularly unaware of it. It took 80 cowboys, using riding horses, motor scooters, airplanes and four-wheel drive vehicles to finally capture him. Old Whitey was a mule. Now mules are considered finished and ancient when they reach their twenties. But someone had neglected to tell Old Whitey this and he was somewhere between 53 and 55 when he was captured. He'd been used as a pack mule for the Union Pacific Railroad in 1915, lost track of after his owner died, and was forgotten. Then someone spotted him in 1961, found the UP brand on his furry neck, let him go, and came back to report the incredible; Old Whitey was still alive. Whitey was a legend by now, but nobody ever really expected to see him again. Around 1966 someone did. That's when the National Mustang Association and the Nevada Horsemen's Association sponsored the strange roundup, to see if it were actually he.

Old Whitey was spotted from the air and in fast company. He was running with eight mustangs and although he was probably older than all of them put together, he outran them all—until someone managed to put a lasso around his neck. His old coat was so long the UP brand wasn't visible but it could be felt. It was Old Whitey all right. His teeth were so worn and slanted they missed meeting by a half inch. But incredibly, he seemed to be as fit as ever! The cowboys let a small boy ride him for a few yards. Then they gently took his lasso off and turned him loose again.

The reason for his longevity is anybody's guess. Some think it is due to his freedom. Some think it's because he'd never had much opportunity to over-eat. But it could be that he had an unquenchable zest for life and simply did not know enough to quit. He never knew he was a mule; he thought he was a mustang.

He never knew he was a mule; he thought he was a mustang.

Enthusiasm is an almost magical quality that can reach and tap unmeasured stores of emotional energy. Some of the most remarkable recoveries from the most ignominious defeats in history have been because someone had the magical quality and the ability to trigger enthusiasm in others.

Churchill had it. He came on the stage at the worst possible moment and he did not attempt to say everything was all right when everything wasn't; he made no bones about what lay ahead, but he seemed to positively relish the prospect of somehow getting *through* what lay ahead—and victoriously. And he transmitted this outrageously enthusiastic attitude to all of Britain and America.

FDR did the same thing. In the face of what seemed like certain defeat he cried out to a distraught nation, "We have nothing to fear but fear itself!" And it worked!

It was not their oratory alone that accomplished these feats. It was their enthusiasm that sparked emotions and released the necessary emotional energy to get the job done.

It's true that enthusiasm makes leaders. But it is enthusiasm in leaders *and* followers that gets things done.

The intrepid John Welsh absolutely refused to recognize defeat. In the dawn of the reformation, when he knelt on the shores of Scotland with his family and a little band of friends, a more defeated group of people would be hard to come by. A ship was waiting alongside; he was being exiled to France, never to see his native land again. But once in France, with his characteristic enthusiasm he tackled the French language with a vengeance, and was preaching in French in fourteen weeks—not just stumbling through it, *preaching* in it! He posted newfound French friends in various places in his audience, and instructed them to stand, whenever he got his verbs too garbled. They were to remain standing until he slowed down and got them straightened out again.

And when Louis XIII decided to wipe out the protestants and attacked the little French town where Welsh was pastor, and all the town's guns but one had been dismantled, Welsh entered into the fray with enthusiasm that did not recognize defeat. He admonished the gunner to get back to the one gun still in operation, while he himself ran for powder. He scooped up a ladle full, and on his way back to the gun some of the king's artillery knocked the ladle flying from his hand. Now to any

To any ordinary Presbyterian, this would have been considered a call from God to go somewhere else.

ordinary Presbyterian this would have been considered a call from God to go somewhere else, but Welsh was no ordinary Christian, Presbyterian or otherwise. He dashed back to the powder bin, swept off his hat, filled it with powder, ran back to the gun, won the battle and saved the day.

When Dwight L. Moody went over to the Wells Street Mission Sunday School in Chicago and asked them for work to do, they told him to go out and get his own class. He not only got his class, but stuffed his pockets with nuts and candy and pennies and recruited children from all over the city, with bribes, with contests, with prayer, with visitation, with his own *enthusiasm* until he had filled Chicago with Sunday Schools. He was like a huge bearded Pied Piper and the children just followed him into the Sunday Schools and into the arms of God.

And when he preached, the words tumbled out with such enthusiasm he could say "Jerusalem" in one syllable. He called Zaacheus "Zachus" and when his family protested, "Don't say 'Zachus,' it's Zaacheus," he bellowed "I don't have *time* to say 'Zaacheus,' there's too much work to be done!"

When Charles Schwab (whose salary was a million dollars a year) was asked what was the secret of his success he answered, "I consider my ability to arouse enthusiasm among my men the greatest asset I possess."

And for every one of these men there were a thousand who did not lack ability and did not lack opportunity; they just lacked *enthusiasm*.

Now, of course, enthusiasm, like many good and desirable traits has to be backed up with more or less ability, depending upon what good thing you are enthusiastic about, and of course with stick-to-it-iveness. It does take a bit of doing. Enthusiasm without follow-through is ineffective; some people use up all their steam in talking. "She has great ideas," someone was heard to remark, "but she never carries them through." Much enthusiasm "dies a-borning" this way.

121

If John Welsh had given up on his French verbs, or if Moody had gone out and gotten his first class of boys and then just let them languish, history would have to be rewritten.

"But," we cry, "I'm not up to all this bubbly-business and all this leaping about." Ah, there is the fallacy. Enthusiasm is *not* all bubbly-bubbly and leaping about at all. Enthusiasm is an *aura*, an attitude, and some of the most quiet people are the most enthusiastic, get the things done, and get the rest of us to believe in something and to be willing to work for it. It is, as we have said, a *magical quality* and it might manifest itself in just twinkling eyes and a quiet smile and a face alight with the joy of living and the love of God.

And now we have to face a hard fact.

Some of us are just not enthusiastic and there is absolutely nothing we can do about it. We are not enthusiastic by temperament; our genes and chromosomes and heritage simply did not give us that trait. Or our upbringing conditioned us beyond repair. And for the life of us we cannot conjure it up or fake it when it is not there.

If you are not enthusiastic there are two things you can do. You can make an effort to change. (You know, the "act and you will *be*" sort of thing.) You've tried it and it does not work? All right, accept yourself as you are, and don't flagellate yourself over it; you will only make it worse. Just make up your mind not to be a wet blanket, casting gloom over the *other* fellow's enthusiasm. If you can at least manage this, you will be making a contribution to humanity of inestimable worth.

A saga of enthusiasm

IT WOUND UP being a great Christian Conference.* But it started with a mountain.

Once upon a time there was a mountain. Of course there are thousands of mountains—and there was nothing to distinguish this one from any other—except that in 1876, a group of men, from various walks of life had climbed to its summit one Memorial Day, and knelt in prayer and dedicated it to God. Now once that's done, no mountain can ever be the same again.

In any life that's been dedicated to God, things begin to happen. And it's no different with a mountain.

Nothing happened right away—but mountains

*Forest Home, founded by Dr. Henrietta C. Mears, Director of Christian Education, Hollywood Presbyterian Church.

have the patience of the aged—and a quarter of a century later—which is nothing to a mountain—an itinerate preacher from a Congregational church went up there, and founded a camp. His name was H. J. Culver, and he had a dream and he worked to back it up.

There was a little log cabin in the center, with tents all around, and a Mrs. Bangs who baked inimitable Parker House rolls. And there were evening campfires and messages from God's Word. The dream began to take shape.

And then the dream began to grow, and there were buildings instead of tents—the Forest Home Hotel—and cabins. It was called the "Forest Home Outing Company." It was at the end of the road, and it took eight hours to get there, by stagecoach.

And then Mr. Culver died, and the dream died with him. The Forest Home Outing Company was sold to a Mr. Durant and he used it as a recreation center and vacation resort and for many years the dream lay dormant.

"Something explosive will have to happen," thought the mountain. "Something *earthshaking*."

And something earthshaking did. Henrietta Mears heard about it. And after Henrietta Mears heard about a mountain—no mountain could ever be the same.

The mountain had been waiting for some years— and for some years, Henrietta Mears had been looking for a place to take her young people. It was just a question of time for God to bring the two things together.

When the realtor phoned Miss Mears, she called

Dr. Cyrus Nelson* and they drove out to see it. And then Miss Mears did the most inconsistent thing in her life. They drove up—and in—and circled around the Forest Home Hotel—and came back out again—and went home.

It was the first time in her life that Henrietta Mears did not get out

walk in

feel

look

snoop

ask

and stare

—until the last smidgen of her insatiable curiosity was satisfied.

She went home and called the Irwin Realtor Company.

"Irwin Realtor Company? May I speak with Mr. Irwin?" And aside to Dr. Nelson, "Honestly. I don't know what's come *over* that man. I asked him to keep his eye open for a camp—something *reasonable*. He's gone beyond the realm of possibility. He's—hello? Mr. Irwin? Henrietta Mears. Yes—just got back. Mr. Irwin—that's impossible. I thought, a little camp, you know, being sold to settle an estate. Did I?—why *no*. We didn't even get out of the car. Why it's absolutely imposs—what's the bank value? Three seventy five? You mean three hundred seventy-five *thousand*. Well don't just toss off '375' like that. When you name a figure like that, you pause for a moment of silence. Mr. Irwin—this may be news to the Republicans—but no matter how

*President of Gospel Light Publications.

euphemistically they put it—we're in the midst of a *depression*. Yes. It's impossible. Why, it's *impossible*."

But they did take an option. And the winter wore on and it looked more impossible as the months went by. So they dropped the option and postponed the dream and planned a trip around the world.

And the mountain? Well if we were trying to be facetious, and we're not, we'd say the mountain had a fit. Because it did have a flood, a devastating flood that almost wiped out the canyon but miraculously left the camp itself virtually untouched. But the devastation everywhere else! Down came torrents of water and tons of debris.

And down came something else.

Dr. Nelson and Ethel Mae Baldwin, Miss Mears' assistant, were at her home when the news came. Mr. Irwin phoned about it. Miss Mears went to the phone.

"Hello? Yes—Mr. Irwin." She held her hand over the mouthpiece. "Eth—Cy, where'd Ethel Mae go? Tell her to come back. It's Mr. Irwin." And back into the phone—"Mr. Irwin? How *are* you. Yes. We've been reading about the flood. Mmmmm. I know. Redlands—and San Berdu—awful. Mmmmmmmm." She listened a moment. Dr. Nelson waited. Ethel Mae who had come back into the room waited.

"We're going around the world," said Miss Mears into the phone. "Well—my sister Margaret—and Dave Cowie he's one of my college boys. Well he *was*. He's a pastor now. And Ethel Mae—and Mr. Bowers. And me of course. Well. I just thought I'd

128

tag along. You know how I hate to miss anything. We're going—hm? Forest Home?"

She covered the mouthpiece again. "Forest Home, Cy." Then back into the phone. "Price is down? Mr. Irwin, that price is so out of reach that down a few thousand isn't going to make any difference. When you're talking in figures like three hundred seventy-five thousand dollars. It's Impossible. What's that? It's down to *thirty* thousand? That's imposs—credible!" She covered the mouthpiece quickly and hissed, "Thirty thousand dollars, he said." They all stared at each other. Then she dived back into the mouthpiece again with sort of a swoop. "Mr. Irwin. Say that again."

They waited. She listened. And covered the mouthpiece again. "That's what he said," she told them, and went back to business. "Mr. Irwin, when can we go up and look at it?"

"You mustn't seem too anxious," hissed Dr. Nelson.

"Hm?" she whispered back.

"You mustn't seem too anxious."

"Oh. You're right. Mustn't seem too anxious." Then back into the phone.

"How about tomorrow at five? No—five *AM*. We can leave in time to have breakfast up there. I'll call Dr. McClennen and Mr. Hormel and the rest. All right. I'll let you know. G'bye, Mr. Irwin."

She hung up and looked at them. "Why're you looking at me like that? What's wrong with 5 AM? You think they won't want to go up that early? Why *of course* they'll want to go. There's nothing like early morning mountain air—"

They shrugged. It was no use. She was on the scent.

Next morning she beamed over her breakfast. At Forest Home. At five AM. "Have some more coffee, Dr. McClennen. Isn't this a deeeelicious breakfast? Smell those wheatcakes. MmmmmMMMM. I tell you there's something about early morning mountain air—"

They poured more coffee. And agreed. She was irresistible.

They toured the grounds—and they were overwhelmed. All the things they'd dreamed about were there. A pool—a tiny golf course—equipment—a store—a dining room—a post office—bedding—a stream with trout fishing—everything!

They went home and prayed it through. Everyone felt the same.

They were all at her home the next night, talking it over.

"Well we're all definitely convinced," she said. "The Lord wants us to have this place."

"What about the trip?" said Dr. Nelson, throwing in a clinker and already knowing she'd throw it back.

"What trip?" she said.

"The trip around the world," he said.

"Oh. *That* trip. Well. What do you think?" And she answered her own question. "We just can't *go*, that's all. You know we can't go. This is more important. We've been asking the Lord for this for *years*."

They already knew, but it was fun to throw clinkers in and watch her throw them out.

"Is Dave Cowie back from the east yet?" she said and she got up and began to pace, *willing* Dave Cowie back from the east. A childlike excitement had crept into her and was busting out all over, a hurry-hurry-and-isn't-this-great-and-let's-get-to-it sort of thing that spilled out all over everybody. "Won't he be thrilled," she said, "just absolutely thri—"

And the phone rang.

"Maybe that's Dave now," she said, her voice high, with gravel creeping into it, which always meant that it would go up and up, words tumbling and telescoping together, into incoherent enthusiasm. She plunged toward the phone and picked it up, all in one gesture.

"Hello? Dave? Where *are* you? The airport? Can you come right out? Take a ca—Dave. You're not going around the world. No, none of us is. We've got Forest Home. *Forest Home*. We're going to buy it. Yes. They came down on the price and they came down on the down payment and we've been up to see it and oh, Dave, it's just—" and she went into a rhapsody of description nobody could understand and wound up with—"it's just *tremendous* what the Lord is doing. It's just—hm? Where're we going to get the down payment? Well. We're each responsible for a thousand dollars. Hm? Well where's the money you were going around the world with? Well there's your thousand dollars. What's the problem?"

That was the beginning.

They scrubbed and cleaned and pounded and pulled out stumps and painted and blasted and pounded and sawed. First conference? Family conference of course. First shopper and general overseer? Henrietta's sister Margaret. In a Model A Ford. First manager? Cy Nelson. First cook? *Everybody*. And Miss Mears? She organized committees, wrote up advertising, acted as chief counselor, did the phoning, and yes, scrubbed and cooked, too. And rounded up the strays—

"Boys!" she shouted one night standing outside a cabin, shivering in her housecoat. "It's one thirty in the morning. You need your rest and we need our rest. This is ridiculous! Now I want no more nonsense. I want absolute silence. Or you'll all go home in the morning!"

There was absolute silence.

She walked away, muttering, incredibly weary physically, incredibly alive otherwise—"The idea. They need their rest. Nobody likes fun any more than I do. But this is ridiculous." And she stopped, leaned against a tree—and chuckled. Then she looked up. And listened. And listened. To the night. "Dear heavenly Father," she said, "put your hand on the life of every boy in that cabin. I claim every life for thee—" She fished for her handkerchief in her housecoat pocket. None. She wiped her eyes on her sleeve. "They're such *noisy* boys, Lord. They've got so much *initiative*. They'll make such *wonderful* ministers—"

She was right about initiative. The boys had sandwiched themselves between mattresses—a mattress, a boy, a mattress, a boy—and stacked themselves to the ceiling. And they all but died, getting

They're such noisy boys, Lord. They've got so much initiative. They'll make such wonderful ministers.

unstacked without any noise. None of them wanted to be sent home.

And so things went on.

She trod the soil of Forest Home—and like Joshua—claimed every inch for God. She climbed to a minor peak one day, where there was nothing but wilderness, and said to those around her—"I see a Lodge, right—there. And a lake. A veritable Eden. We could call it 'Lakeview.'"

Everyone nodded.

"Well?" she said. "Can we bring up some bulldozers—and how soon?"

And that's the way it was. That's the way it always was with her. You didn't just talk about it. You *did* it.

The mountain looked down from its major peak and thought, "Bless my bones—eh—stones. I'm

My very snowcaps aren't safe anymore.

dealing with a woman who moves mountains. My very snowcaps aren't safe anymore."

Well they were. She did leave those—for a magnificent view. But bulldozers did lop off a bit of the minor peak and soon there was a beautiful lodge and there were cabins and homes and yes, an artificial lake.

Forest Home grew and often they went right up to the deadline on payments and turned their own personal bank accounts inside out but they never missed a payment and they were never overdue and Forest Home became one of the greatest conference grounds on the West Coast.

Henrietta Mears had enthusiasm with stick-to-itiveness and this kind of enthusiasm bulldozed down every obstacle in its path.

No one could resist it. The boys in that cabin all became ministers and great Christian laymen, the beginning of a long long line.

In the path of her enthusiasm no one was ever the same again.

Even the mountain.

How is your C.Q.?*

*Communication Quotient

LET'S ASSUME that we have diligently looked at our personalities and plucked this out and added that attitude and even thrown in some enthusiasm to make it all come out right. And we still have difficulty in getting along with people. It leaves us baffled and defeated. Could it be that we're just *not getting across?*

What a tremendous relief if it *were* something like that; we are saints after all, we just can't *communicate* and all this fuss has been about nothing.

This is the lazy way out. If you've read this far and have a brand-new set of attitudes it's a waste to keep them all to yourself.

Communication is to make known, to give to another, to impart. A communicating hallway connects two rooms, so to say "We really connected!" is not as slangy as it might seem.

A staggering percentage (a neat way to avoid statistics) of failures in business and Christian work stems from poor communication. The foreman thinks "watch those machines" and the manager thinks "watch that budget" and the workers think "watch that clock" and the Sunday School superintendent thinks "watch that attendance" and the teacher thinks "watch that curriculum" and the pastor thinks "preach that sermon" and nobody thinks "communicate with those people."

Modern business and government have discovered that a myriad of mistakes, time lost, money lost, hard feelings, and problems that are legion, are due to improper communication. And modern business and government spend millions on it each year.

And from this fancy gobbledegook (a word derived, aptly enough, from the sound a turkey cock makes and meaning inflated, involved and obscure verbiage) that was in a report from the Government's Department of Housing and Urban Development, they need to spend a few million more:

"Action-oriented orchestration of innovative inputs, generated by escalation of meaningful decision-making dialogue, focusing on multi-linked problem-complexes, can maximize the vital thrust toward a nonalienated and viable infrastructure."

"Escalation of meaningful decision-making dialogue" undoubtedly means that someone had a committee meeting. You think this cannot happen in a church? More "escalation of meaningful decision-

138

making dialogue focusing on multi-linked problem-complexes" have been perpetrated in churches and Christian organizations than anywhere else. The problem is, the "action-oriented orchestration" usually gets lost in the shuffle and the result is a cacophony of noise instead of integrated instrumentation.

In any case, they are serious about it, and send their executives scurrying off to learn how to communicate, and that's a good start. It must be important.

It *is* important. Can you imagine how horrendous it would be if all communications broke down? The results are unimaginable. It is exactly what happened at the tower of Babel.

I witnessed a little drama once, when communications broke down on a smaller scale, actually it was a light and frothy little piece, and it amused me no end.

I was in a supermarket drugstore—the kind where you go in to buy an aspirin and by the time you wander through the bicycles, ceramics, do-it-yourselves, cosmetics, curtain rods, hardware, clothing, ad nauseum, you come to the checking-out desk with a cart full of stuff you did not want, and with any luck, your aspirin.

I found myself behind a nice young man, and off to my left were two children—a boy and his younger sister, who were apparently his offspring.

The man was going through one of those nightmares-come-true—a thing you dream about but hope never happens to you, like being caught going down a thoroughfare without your clothes—he had given (or thought he had given) the clerk a twenty dollar bill and she was giving him change for a ten.

Meanwhile, the two kids had dived into the freezer nearby and had come up with two Popsicles which he had told them to pick out for themselves.

The little boy unpeeled his. It was green. The little girl unpeeled hers. It was orange. Then a look of covetousness appeared in her eyes.

"I want a green one," she said.

"Daddy, she wants a green one!" the little boy reported.

"I want a green one!" she echoed.

But the daddy and the clerk were otherwise occupied.

"Ma'am, I gave you a twenty," he said.

"No—you gave me a ten," she said.

"She wants a green one!" said the little boy.

"I want a green one!" wailed the little girl, as she dropped her orange one.

"Kids!" he implored, "Just a minute." Then he turned to the clerk. "Ma'am, I *know* I gave you a twenty. See? I have nothing else in my wallet. And I know I had a twenty."

"She wants a green one!" said the little boy.

"I want a green one!" wailed the little girl, as she picked up her orange one and wiped it on her jacket sleeve.

"Kids!" implored the daddy. And he again turned to the clerk, this time in desperation. "Ma'am I *know* I gave you a twenty. Look, I just had this twenty and I—"

"She wants a green one!"

"I want a—"

"KIDS!"

I stood there, watching, my eyes on swivels.

"Look sir, we put the bill on the *outside* of the register before we make the change. Here it is. A ten. And we—"

"I want a green one!" crunched the little girl as she took a bite of her orange one.

"KIDS!!!!!"

And then came the moment of truth. He explored his wallet again and came up fiery red, torn between embarrassment and relief.

"Oh good grief," he said, and pulled out a twenty. "My twenty was here in my secret compartment. Oh good grief. I'm sorry—"

"I want a green one!" bellowed the little girl as she dropped her orange one and picked it up again.

"That's okay," said the clerk. "We all make mistakes."

"Good grief, I'm sorry—"

"Daddy, I want a green one!"

And at last he turned his attention to them.

"What do you want?" he said.

I stood rooted to the spot. I had seen all.

"She wants a green one," said the little boy.

"I want a green one," said the little girl.

And before my horrified eyes, he said, "Well put it back and take a *green* one!"

She did.

Oh good grief.

Should I step forth with the grim facts I knew were being held in abeyance? Should I disclose the hidden evidence that would straighten out the whole case? Or should I keep my peace?

I decided that discretion was the better part of valor and kept silent. They went happily on their way. Then I stepped up to the clerk.

"Don't look now," I hissed, "but there is a very dog-eared partially eaten and very *very* dirty orange Popsicle in the case. You'd better take it out."

She did.

And we both laughed. "The poor man was distraught enough," I said. "I'll be glad to pay for the Popsicle." She declined. The Popsicle was "on the house."

I went away very thoughtful. I had witnessed some minor chaos in which nobody had communicated with anybody and forevermore, some of the pertinent facts would be undisclosed to that harassed daddy. I had, in a sense, been omniscient for the moment; I had possession of facts that nobody else did; I knew the denouement. It gave me a feeling of awe.

I knew, also, something of this business of communication. It was a thoughtful lesson. I chewed on it all the way back to my car.

Communication. Something beyond our control? Yes, I thought—partially. For there will always be undisclosed facts. I can try, I can probe, I can honestly practice understanding, I can even try to examine the other fellow's problems and with much morbid introspection dissect myself, but there will *always* be facts I cannot get ahold of. Such a dreary business. How are we to solve it?

142

Well we can't entirely, for we "see ourselves darkly, as in a glass" and we can hardly hope to see others any more sharply; God keeps that prerogative for himself. But can we make a try? Let's dissect it from a human viewpoint and see what we come up with.

We see communication in terms of the mere mechanics involved. You talk—I listen. I write—you read. You make a map—I follow directions. You make a sign with your eyes at me from across a room—I get the message and make a sign back, and we both understand. Up to the best of our ability we have communicated.

But communication goes beyond the mere transmittal of messages. It delves deeper, to both our joy and consternation; it involves the whole individual. In several different ways. *And on many different levels of awareness.* We could say "Selah" right here and be afraid to ever venture out again, if we really thought about it. It is enough to frighten us into a hermit's existence for the rest of our lives.

Communication is concerned with all situations involving "meaning."

It is concerned with your attempts to:

Express yourself to others, who you are and what you mean.

I was in the Middle East once, packed in a car with some friends and an Arab guide who was a jolly chap—a bit fragrant perhaps with the accumulation of the by-products of hard labor and the singular lack of cognition of the beauties-of-the-bath—(We took turns sitting next to him; no one could stand it for long)—but jolly, nonetheless. And

143

willing. And able. But he could not speak English. So you see right off that we were going to have problems in communication. He had been instructed to stop whenever we bade him so we could take pictures. Well we started off on our little side trip and began to climb the most mountainous country I have ever seen. We scaled undreamed-of heights with mountains still higher to our front and left and with a sheer drop of practically eternity to our right. And this happy chap just drove on with abandon, his hand gleefully pressed to his horn in supreme confidence that anyone coming would just naturally get out of his way. If ever there was a candidate for the Optimist Club, he was it. Finally I said to him in a high voice* "What is your name?" trying to be friendly and to get his mind on something else to slow him down. Immediately he swerved to the side of the road with great screeching of brakes barely missing plunging us into the abyss below. We sat there in silence for a moment. What had happened? What had I done? We tapped him timidly on the shoulder. "Go on," we said, gesticulating, to indicate what we meant. He did. A moment later I tried again. "Do you—" that's as far as I got. We screeched to the perilous edge again. And we waited. We tapped him again. We went on. And then I knew. There was no sense trying to be friendly or to establish a rapport with him. He knew one order. To stop when we spoke, so we could take pictures. We were absolutely "out of communication." After that we did not speak to him

*My voice always goes up to a treble when I am nonplused or upset or frightened.

144

unless we *wanted* to take pictures, and that was that. As far as we were concerned he had a pristine mind, completely unsullied by any attempt of mine to put anything more upon it; we took pictures or we did not take pictures, and he was concerned with nothing else.

I had the same problem with another Arab, this one the owner of a very affectionate camel that nuzzled him in the neck and was really quite icky about it. (This surprised me, for camels' faces had always looked to me like somebody's Victorian aunt who had just been shocked by an unspiritual remark.) I was atop the camel and he noticed that I held lightly to just the front horn of the saddle instead of grasping both ends. "Ah, mad*am*," he said, giving the last syllable just enough emphasis to send my spirits soaring, "I perceive that you know how to ride a camel." "No," I said modestly, "but I know how to ride a horse." The truth of the matter was that though I had ridden horses, it was with much fear and trembling and any horse who had me on his back knew he was the master. I had a history of dangling stirrups and frantic posting

145

and the horse was always glad when I got off. But I neglected to communicate this, so he, in all good faith, flicked his whip against his camel and shouted, "Heigh-ho Silver, awaaaaaaaay!" And the camel did.

Well camels, once they get the hang of it, get into the swing of things and keep with you very nicely, and we got off to a sporting stop in a matter of fifty yards or so.

In both cases I was unable to express myself and explain what I meant.

Communication is concerned with your attempts to:

Understand the expression of others—to know who they are and what they mean.

This is an area in which we make more mistakes, and find more excuses than we care to admit.

"Why didn't he explain it more carefully?"

"If that's what he meant why didn't he say so?"

"Did she expect me to read her mind?"

"How was I supposed to know he meant that?"

"Well if only she had explained it, I wouldn't have bungled it so badly. She just mumbles and rambles and I don't know what she's talking about half the time."

"Why can't he just say what he means? He talks in circles."

"All she had to do was *say* so. How was I supposed to know what she meant?"

And so we go on blaming the other fellow, forgetting that half the burden is ours. The little boy who said, "But Mommy, I *did* tell you but you were listening in a hurry," had a case. More often than not we don't understand others because we don't make enough of an effort. In our business we can always say, "Would you mind putting this in a memo so I'll be sure I got it right?" but we'd look pretty silly carrying this over into our private lives. We might get things straight, but we'd be fresh out of both friends and family in a month, and be left communicating only with ourselves. Which brings us to the next point.

Communication is concerned with your attempts to:

Understand yourself and what you mean.

I went to a friend once. "I have been put in the wrong, and very unjustly," I said in my low even voice, "and I find the situation intolerable." And I told him about it.

"What are you afraid of?" he said.

"But you don't understand," I said patiently in my middle-sized voice. And I explained it again, repeating some fine points he might have missed.

"What are you afraid of?" he said.

"You misunderstand me," I said in my middle-sized big voice. "I am not afraid. I am righteously indignant. And I do not intend to stand for it."

"What are you afraid of?" he said.

"I am not afraid," I said in my big voice. "I'm angry."

"What are you afraid of?" he said.

"I am not afraid," I said in my great big voice. "I'm FURIOUS!"

There was a long pause.

"I'm afraid," I said in my little tiny voice. "I'm afraid because I ran into just such a situation once

147

before and I failed and I'm afraid I might fail again. I don't want to ruin this relationship."

"That's better," he said.

"I think I can straighten it out now," I said in my middle-size voice. "Thanks for listening."

Communication is concerned with your attempts to understand yourself and what you mean.

There is an old Chinese poem that goes something like this:

There's no end of talking,
And there is no use in talking,
For there's no end of the things in the heart.

SYMBOLIC COMMUNICATION

Symbolic communication is the kind we are all familiar with—talking, writing, making signs and gestures, drawing pictures, and all the obvious ways we have to let the other fellow know we're here. It enables us to become better informed and to inform others. But like all good things God has given us, we can run it into the ground, mix it up, use it to deceive ourselves and others, and misuse it in general.

There is no end to the ways we can distort communication; our talents in this direction are staggering. But here are a few.

We can give a person a label. And, if it's a false one, the harm it will do him is incalculable. One of the most horrendous examples of this, is the label "traitor." We read in the papers that a man is one. He may go on trial to prove that he isn't and be completely acquitted and exonerated, but forever more when you hear his name you think "traitor."

148

To a lesser degree you can do the same thing to a person by giving him the label of "liar." A child can go from grade to grade with this label passed along with him; he may have stopped being one years before but the label is still sticking to him like feathers to tar.

Or the label of "failure."

We moved from one state (where reading was taught by flash card) to another (where reading was taught by phonetics) when son number one was in the middle of first grade. When we walked into the lobby of the new school we heard a screaming shrew on the second floor lambasting her class collectively and individually for its latest infraction. "I hope she's not your teacher," I muttered good-naturedly. Of all the words I have ever eaten, those were the ones that gave me the most indigestion.

For it turned out she was.

Most teachers fortunately have teachers' hearts. But a few of them unfortunately are counterparts of small-town sheriffs. She promptly branded son number one a failure (he was quite unable to make the shift into phonetics) and one term and two

She promptly branded son number one a failure.

149

facial tics later turned him over to the next teacher with his "label" written on his report card. He figuratively sat down by the side of the road and quit trying. No amount of encouragement at home availed.

This "label" followed him from grade to grade and even jumped the state line and found its way to a new school. We walked into the new room to face his new third grade teacher, his "label" carefully written on his old report card, and all over his face. We stood before her like two failures are wont to stand, heads down, facial tics a-jumping* and awaited her verdict. I don't recall, but it seems to me I expected to at least be put in stocks. She glanced cursorily at the offending card, got quickly to her feet—and grinned. Then she tore the card up, not dramatically, but with a masterpiece of understatement as if she were just tossing off something that was of absolutely no importance. And she stretched her hand across her desk to shake hands with my tic-ridden failure-riddled miserable child. "We're not going to look back," she said matter-of-factly, "we're going to take it from *here*. And you're going to be at least a B student. I know it."

Like Spring, son number one "busted out all over." I saw a new birth, emotionally speaking, right before my eyes. He looked up at her with blind adoration and his lop-sided grin was something to behold. The wretched "label" lay in forgotten pieces on her desk blotter, never to be mentioned again. And he became a B student because,

*By this time I had picked up a mini-tic.

well it was the gentlemanly thing to do; you just couldn't let a person down who had *that* kind of faith in you.

God bless you, Mrs. Grogan, wherever you are. Amen.

We can deceive by telling the absolute truth. It's easy. Just leave something out. There was a captain of a ship who, for some undisclosed reason, wanted to get rid of his first mate. He did not abuse his victim or malign him. He told the absolute truth. Every three or four days he made an entry in his log—"The first mate was sober today." The first mate was sober every day but the implication did its deadly work and the first mate was subsequently discharged.

I used to speak at Executive Dinner Clubs. In a certain large city I had lunch with the editor of the paper who was an officer in the club and who always wrote up the evening's program for the next day's edition. Somehow we did not get on well. It is always a bit of a jolt when we find some one doesn't like us, though we know we should know better— but I knew he did not like me and I left him, wishing that someone else was going to do that write-up. That evening I told the audience that the evening would be a light one, that I did not have slides or a pointer, and I promised not to have an "expert" opinion on anything. This good gentleman reported me truthfully. He just left out one word. "Miss Barrett," he said, "did not have an opinion on anything," and thereby shot me down in flames.

Sometimes we hear but our minds refuse to accept what we heard.

Son number one was down from the mountains for the day one time. He'd had my car, but now I needed it, so I was going to drive him back to his summer job. "Why don't we take son number two along?" I said, "it'll be fun to all be together."

"We can't do that," he said, "there won't be room for the goats."

"Oh," I said and started down the hallway toward my bedroom. Halfway there I turned and walked back to him. "I thought you said goats," I said laughing. He didn't laugh back. "You didn't say goats, of course," I said, laughing again. He didn't laugh back. "You *did* say goats!" I said. And he nodded his head ruefully.

"You have goats out there?"

"Mother I told you I had goats when I came home."

"In my car? In my nice car you have *goats?*"

"But Mother I told you. You even saw me warming their bottles."

"Baby goats?"

And then I remembered. He *had* been warming bottles at that. Could I have actually been that preoccupied? Incredible. He had to be kidding. I rushed out to the car.

It was true. Two twin baby goats, all black, and so incredibly adorable that all my lifetime prejudices against goats crumpled.

I'd heard him all right, but my mind had refused to accept it.

Sometimes we don't really mean what we're saying.

I was putting son number two to bed one night

when he was about six. I opened his bottom drawer to get something and there in a T shirt that had been bunched up to make a nest, was a family of brand new field mice. I did what any red-blooded American mother would do under such circumstances. I slammed the drawer shut and screamed.

"Steve!" I said. "What on earth are these hideous things doing in there?"

He was standing behind me with a half cup of milk in his hand and a medicine dropper. "Eli," (Eli was the gardener) "ran over their nest with the electric lawn mower," he said. "He didn't mean to. It was an accident. The mother got cut up in little pieces too short to hang up. She just sorta disappeared. So these are orphans."

"But you can't keep them here," I wailed. "They're *rodents*. They carry *disease*." I put my finger in his cup of milk. "You can't—(hey, go warm that milk; you'll kill them this way with cold milk) —you can't keep them here."

He trotted off to warm the milk. I opened the drawer again. They were incredibly tiny with no hair at all, their skin transparent, their little insides showing through. I couldn't eat a Vienna sausage for years afterward.

He returned, squatted alongside me by the open drawer, turned one of the little things over on its back and began to drop milk in its little face.

"These things are *dirty*," I continued. "They carry —(hey you'll drown them with that. It's too much. We need a hypodermic needle)—they carry disease!"

Minutes later we were back squatting again with a hypo syringe and a needle whose point I'd broken off with plyers. "Squeeze his cheeks in together to open his mouth," I said. And I squeezed my cheeks in to show him. Now we were working together seriously like a team of surgeons. "You absolutely cannot keep these dirty things," I said softly, landing a drop of milk with expert precision. "They carry—*squeeze*. That's it. They carry disease. Of all the hairbrained things to do—*squeeze*. That's better. Good. Now we have it. He's had enough. Turn the next one over. Good."

Well the upshot was, we set the alarm and got up every two hours all night, warming milk and squeezing cheeks and opening mouths. And each time I did it I picked up my senseless monologue where I'd left off. Son number two wasn't fooled. He knew I didn't mean what I was saying. The mice never found it out.*

I received a phone call once from a friend who was going with us and several other families to a picnic. "We can't go Saturday," she said. "Jack" (her husband) "forgot that he'd promised his Sunday School class he'd take them to the ball game."

"What?" I wailed, and, "Can't he take them some other time?"

"I told him that," she said. "But he says he made a promise and he feels he should keep it. They depend on what you say, you know. He doesn't want to let them down."

I hung up, disappointed. But I had to admit grudgingly that Jack's junior boys would be glad that when he said something, he meant it.

---

*The poor little things were mercifully dead in the morning. We'd killed them with kindness.

Sometimes we listen in gaps.

I was in a hotel in Salina, Kansas once, propped up in bed with my portable typewriter on my knees, struggling to meet a deadline for a book. As I was writing, a sound truck went by. And a voice boomed out, filling the whole town it seemed, "BOMBING PLANES ARE HEADED FOR SALINA. GO TO YOUR BASEMENTS. DO NOT GO OUT INTO THE STREETS," and then ended with "THIS IS A TEST ONLY. THIS IS A TEST ONLY."

"Oh," I muttered, enormously relieved, and went back to my writing. The voice went on but I was oblivious to it.

Moments later I was brought up with a jolt.

"THERE IS A TORNADO HEADED FOR SALINA," boomed the ominous voice again. "GO TO YOUR BASEMENTS. DO NOT GO OUT INTO THE STREETS. GO TO YOUR BASEMENTS."

I whisked the typewriter off my lap, threw the covers back and leapt to my feet. A tornado! I'd read about them but I'd never been *in* one before. Good grief! I stood there a moment in panic and unbelief. What would I take? I threw on my leather coat, grabbed my typewriter and manuscript. I forgot my purse. I started for the door. Then I stopped. Why not phone downstairs and find out just how serious this was? I picked up the receiver.

"DO NOT USE YOUR PHONE!" boomed the voice. I dropped the phone. I thought the man was right at my shoulder and had seen what I'd done. I started for the door again, and then—

"THIS IS A TEST ONLY. THIS IS A TEST ONLY," boomed the voice.

Words cannot describe my humiliation as I unloaded my accoutrements and crawled back into bed. Of course. I should have known. They *had* been talking about "tests only" a few moments before. But I'd "tuned out" and there was a gap in my listening and when I "tuned in" again I had completely lost track of the message.

Sometimes we add to what we heard.

That night I spoke at the Knife-and-Fork Club of Salina. Next to me sat their District Attorney, an affable man he, and a very good listener. So I was foolish enough to tell him what I had done.

I left town the next day thinking my secret was safe. But a few days later he sent me an account of it in the Salina paper. The heading was "SHE HAD HEARD OF TORNADOS" and the account was amusing; in fact it was much more amusing than it had been in the first place. It had me with my hair in curlers, rushing down to the lobby! He had added to what he'd heard. In this case it made the story ever so much better and did no harm and I was immensely amused and delighted. But adding to what we've heard can be dangerous contraband sometimes, and a talent we would do well to bury.

Sometimes we give the wrong impression.

I was speaking once, I don't remember where, when I spied a gentleman in the audience who was looking at me as if he'd been baptized in vinegar. The air was filled with merriment and joy, but no matter how I tried to win him over and coax him to get into the spirit of the thing, he was implacable. Right to the bitter end.

Afterward, I was happily engaged in my favorite pastime—the joy of talking with people, meeting old friends and making new ones—when out of the periphery of my vision I saw *him* approaching.

"Oh good grief," I thought. "He's coming up." I wanted to run.

I turned to him, prepared for the worst. He thrust out his hand, and with the same expression he'd worn all evening, said, "I never enjoyed anything so much in my life." I very nearly hugged him in relief.

We make the wrong impression on others and they make the wrong impression on us, and most of the time it's nobody's fault, because most of us just can't say what we mean or look what we mean and it's a hopeless tangle of misunderstood words, attitudes and facial expressions.

Sometimes we don't put our ideas across with directness.

We had a cat once, and we named him Timothy

And then he got married and had a litter of kittens and we changed his name to Timothy Lulu.

Barrett and then he got engaged and we were suspicious and then he got married and had a litter of kittens and we were sure and we changed his name to Timothy Lulu Barrett and then he got old and was just neuter gender, but no matter what he was or did we adored him to the end. He just had a personality that was almost human no matter what his gender or his age.

Anyhow, Timothy Lulu had a habit of sleeping under the stove while I was cooking dinner. It was warm there, and he'd made it a refuge from the trials and vagaries of his weary day.

Whenever I cooked hamburger for dinner (which was often for we were tight in the budget department and I kept my sons blissfully ignorant of what a real steak was for years; protein is protein—why be fussy about it?) I had this irresistible impulse to roll up a little ball of it and place it about six inches from Timothy Lulu's nose. Then I'd dash to where my sons were playing in the other part of the house.

"Kids!" I'd hiss. "Want to see something funny?" And they'd come arunning. They'd been long since conditioned to my behavior. It never embarrassed them.*

So we would squat, all three of us, and watch. First Timothy Lulu's top antennae would stand up straight. Then they would almost cross with the impact of the message they'd picked up from the air. Then his whiskers would perk up and wiggle deliciously. Then his whole face would contort in ecstasy and the pure delight of discovery. Then his

*They thought *other* kids' mothers were abnormal and I did my best to keep up this illusion.

paws would twitch. Then he would open his eyes, sleepily at first, and then to their fullest unfathomable depths. And then—

Oh what fun!

He would pounce upon the ball of hamburger with glee. And we would slap each other on the back and laugh with delight and congratulate each other that we had certainly fooled Timothy Lulu again. We'd gotten the idea across to him all right, but by a circuitous route.

By all the laws of common sense it is a good idea to get our ideas across with directness, of course. But there is always the exception to the rule, and sometimes it's a good idea *not* to.

Florence Nightingale knew this. A careful reading of a really good biography of her is a study in executive ability, indeed a study in how to get anything done at all when you're dealing with other people.

I used to think of her as an angel of light, gentle, ethereal, self-sacrificing; comforting soldiers, soothing brows and carrying that lamp all over the place.

It never occurred to me that she was a hardheaded executive, an absolute genius in getting things done.

But she was.

She was certainly all of the other things, too, or she would never have "cast her life away" in such an extravagant gesture of sacrifice. But could she ever get things done!

She got things done with directness—at first. And then the proverbial disenchantment set in and she made enemies—many enemies. They blocked her efforts, they thwarted her in every area, for the truth of the matter was they just did not like her; she was too hard to get along with. Now she could have just folded up or become a termagant, quarreling and bulldozing her way through, "throwing her weight around" and making herself generally hated. The work would get done, but in what a spirit!

Instead, she got things done by circuitous routes, and her resourcefulness knew no end.

She desperately needed A to get something done. But she could not go to A. Somewhere along the line she had ruffled his feelings. Did she give up? She did not. She went to B. "B," she said, "I want this thing done. It is very necessary. Thousands of soldiers' comfort depend upon it. I cannot go to A. He will not listen to me. But if *you* go to A, tell him the plan, make him think it's yours, or better still make him think it's *his*—"

Ah, cagey, that.

She had the sense to know that A would "tune her out" the moment she opened her mouth. She also had the sense to know that the thing had to be done and it did not matter *who* did it.

It is a good idea to put our thinking across with directness, to be sure, but sometimes it is expedient if we do not. It takes a bit of doing, but it can be done.

EMPATHIC COMMUNICATION

Empathic communication is something to reckon with. It's a "feeling tone." For it *is* true that we communicate on several different levels of aware-

wait for the comb out in comparative safety. But the little monster came barging out there, throwing magazines in wild disarray and lunging at us screaming wildly. I was about to gather my purse, leave my money and make my departure, still uncombed, when a stocky blond woman came into the room in curlers, and fixed him with a gelid stare and said, "Sit down." He looked at her nonplused, but only momentarily, and then picked up another magazine to hurl. But she was undaunted. "Sit DOWN," she said, and this time punctuated it by picking him up and sitting him, hard, on a chair. "Now SIT," she said matter-of-factly, and with such authority that I would have obeyed her myself. And she sat down beside him. Well, he stayed sat, but he puckered up and put up a wail that would have called out the militia. We who were there waited, half in relief and half in speculation—obviously a major skirmish was in operation. And as armchair generals do, we all began to silently place our bets, ostensibly still reading our magazines but glancing up periodically, entranced, waiting to see if things would be in our favor.

As he wailed and thrashed, we waited. She calmly picked up a magazine and found a picture and handed it to him and said, "What's this?" He just wailed. "What's this?" she repeated. He hiccoughed and gulped, "That's a cow." "Good," she said, and deftly turned a page and helped him blow his nose in one gesture. "And what's this?" He looked at her speculatively and then back at the picture. "That's a tree," he said, still hiccoughing, but not as violently. "Good," she said, and turned some more pages.

Then, "That's a lady," he said without being asked. "A funny lady." And they both laughed. And then they began to turn pages together, and the hiccoughing stopped and he exclaimed with obvious delight at every new picture and told her what it was. After a few minutes, she got up and said to him, "Now you look at the pictures, you hear? And *stay* here." And she started to move off.

I looked up.* "Your little boy is very bright," I ventured. She looked at me in surprise. "My little boy?" she said. "I don't even know him. I never *saw* the kid before." And before I could reply—"but I know kids. They want discipline. And this kid sure needed it." And she disappeared, leaving us all feeling a little foolish. And he *sat* there.

When his mother finally emerged to claim him, we did not really see her; she seemed scarcely worthy of note. We saw only a thoroughly disciplined child take her hand and go off into the world —his old world—having had one bright and wonderful experience of what life's all about, probably to forget it all too soon.

Now if this were a conjured-up illustration I would say that a lovely soft-voiced lady had whispered in his ear wonderful uplifting and spiritual things, but such is not the case. (I could have had a go at it but I preferred to whine and complain to myself and hide behind my magazine.)

The truth is that the lady who subdued him and charmed him was a brash, matter-of-fact woman who did it in such a way that brooked no nonsense.

---

*I'd been peeking all the time; I just pretended to look up.

But he somehow sensed the "feeling tone" between them. And he knew—in some inexplicable way, that she *liked* him.

I received a note once from son number one's release time Bible school teacher, telling us that he was unhappy. Well, unhappy wasn't exactly what it said. What it actually said was that he was impossible. I did not see the note until just before dinner and as we had a guest, I skipped the whole matter and did not show him by as much as a look that I was upset. After our guest left, I was sitting by the fire when I heard him come down the stairs. He stood in the doorway looking dejected, rejected, a little defiant and just plain scared stiff. "Come on over," I said. He settled himself on the davenport with me, a safe distance away, and I went on looking at the fire. "Want to talk about it?" I said.

"Do you really want to know why I did it?" His voice was thin; he was frightened, bracing himself for something.

"It would help us both if you'd tell me."

"I did it because—" he had turned deadly pale— "I hated you."

"Oh," I said matter-of-factly, "I used to hate my mother, too."

The astonishment on his face was beyond description. "You *did?*"

"Uh huh."

"When? *Why?*"

"Oh different times and the reason wasn't always the same. It never lasted."

I looked at him sideways and I gave him time to digest this before I went on.

"It's natural to hate—sometimes even those we love. But it shouldn't last. It's something you have to give to the Lord right away. If it lasts—then it's wrong."

"Oh." This was apparently such a revelation to him that the relief on his face was almost comical. He told me then, without prodding. It was a routine "teacher's kid" complex. I was teaching Sunday School and had a radio Bible program—and it was all too much responsibility on his shoulders.

"I'm getting over it already," he said finally. "Just talking about it." I agreed with him that the responsibility *was* terrific and told him I'd help him with it all I could, and that God certainly knew all about such things and was more than willing to help us over the rough spots. We prayed about it easily and naturally and without strain. And when he rose to go, he turned to me for a moment before he went upstairs. "D'you know," he said, "you're a very explanatory woman."

I grinned back at him. "Thanks," I said. "But you know if it happens again I'm going to have to punish you. And I warn you, it'll be rough."

"Yup," he said, but without anger. He knew I loved him.

My very first Sunday School class shall always remain the most horrible example of all those wretched levels. Someone called me and asked me to substitute-teach for the summer—a class of girls about thirteen years old or so. And I said, "Who, *me?*" That is, I meant to say it, but no voice came out I was so terrified at the very thought. I looked behind me as Gideon must have, thinking surely the Lord must have meant someone else. I had a women's chatter show on secular radio at the time and was not afraid of a mike or an unseen audience, but the idea of facing a circle of thirteen year old girls was absolutely the most terrifying prospect of my life. Little boys I knew and dogs I knew and radio I knew—but thirteen year old girls —*looking* at me! Well I said yes, and hung up the phone—and put my head down on the desk and cried. I know that seems silly but I suddenly realized that I was about to embark upon the most important calling of my life.

I studied diligently all week and went to Sunday School damp with perspiration, and it wasn't the heat. It was my parasympathetic nervous system, the culprit, working overtime and playing pranks on me.

I entered their Sunday School room like a puppy knowing he is in the front parlor and knowing he does not be'ong there. I began to teach and they looked at me with absolutely blank faces, like fish on chipped ice in a meat market. I would make a point—something I thought was terribly clever or dramatic or profound or thought provoking—and pause to let it sink in and get a reaction. And they would look at each other, still deadpan, then look back at me. My mind would split in two, one half of it on the lesson, the other half thinking, "What in the world are they *saying* to each other?"

At the end of the class hour—(the clock said it was an hour though I have never believed it; it was a millennium and I have been thousand years older ever since)—they got up with great relief and scurried out of the room like young colts just let out of a corral. One of them turned to another as she passed me and said, "Are you coming back next Sunday? We're going to the beach." "We're not going any place," yawned her friend, "but I don't think I'm coming back."

I went home and cried.

What had happened? My lesson had been well prepared and I had given it to God. I suppose the trouble was that I took it right back again for at that time in my life I was a little nervous about God and inclined to think that periodically I had better step in and take over for fear he might not be up to it. We had all communicated all right; on several different levels of awareness. I had communicated to them my terror and they had communicated to me their boredom and though I was teaching and they were quietly listening, there were all those dreadful levels working overtime and actually we were not communicating with any real rapport at all.

Empathic communication all boils down to attitude, which is a deep and profound subject, some of the answers to which I have found on my knees or walking along the beach in the early morning, and many of the answers I am still finding and have yet to find.

In connection with attitude, however, there is a good thing to remember, and it is "positive thinking," a fighting word among us* for we think of it without God, a sort of a do-it-yourself thing that enables us to lift ourselves up by our own boot-

*More spiritual Christians.

straps. But have we ever stopped to think that *with* God it can be one of the most powerful weapons we can have to wield in dealing with others?

I got to thinking about it once and gave it a real try. Son number two wasn't communicating with me. Actually we weren't communicating with each other. Well actually we were at swords points most of the time. I couldn't get through to the little monster no matter what. But this particular morning it came to me as I was praying that instead of trying to get through to him it might be a jolly idea if I tried to get through to myself and change some attitudes. The "oh-how-I-have-prayed-for-you" attitude had to go. I examined the "I-wish-you-were-more-spiritual" attitude.

Out, out, out.

The "After-all-I've-sacrificed-for-you" one was a bit stickier.

"But as long as I've *enjoyed* doing it, Lord," I countered.

No answer.

"But I've never *said* it, not even to myself, in so many words, Lord."

No answer.

All right. Out. If I was going to do this thing I was going to go whole hog. I called son number two to rise and shine,* and went to the kitchen to get his breakfast. And I began my thinking program.

"I love you," I thought. And I laid the slabs of cold bacon in the pan. He sat at the table, taciturn and uncommunicative, his own usual self.

*A bit of an overstatement.

"You are of great worth to me and to God. Do you know what a jolly and wonderful person you are?" And I turned the bacon and broke the eggs in the pan.

"Do you know how much you are loved and appreciated?" And I turned the eggs expertly without breaking the yolks.

"You have given me such joy, from the moment I rocked you in that old chair I bought from the Salvation Army store and painted yellow. And all through the years when you were growing up. I was so delighted at your wit and charm I could hardly believe you belonged to me." Well this was getting a bit icky but I was getting into the spirit of the thing.

The toast popped up and interrupted me for a moment but I went on doggedly. "If I had it all to do over again I would not miss having you for the world. All the stupid things I have done and all the stupid things *we* have done—they don't matter, they don't matter. The thing that matters is that I love you. And I appre—"

"Hey, Mom," he said suddenly, "D'you know what happened in school yesterday?"

I almost dropped his breakfast.

"No, what?" I said. And he told me about it while we ate. Afterward we read the Bible and then I said, "Say, we ought to pray for me this morning. I'm speaking in high school chapel—two thousand students and I feel terribly inadequate by myself."

He looked up and paled visibly. "In Hollywood High?" he said.

"No," I said, "In Burbank High."

"Oh," he said, "Thank God."

I laughed. "I know. You feel pretty silly sitting in a high school audience while your mother's speaking. If it *were* Hollywood High, I wouldn't let on that I even knew you." And he laughed *back*.

Those crazy levels were for real. All you had to do was work them right.

Feeling tones are communicated according to people's personalities and degrees of perception. Some of us are adept at concealing our feelings. Some of us are like "open books." Some of us want to reveal our feelings and can't. Some of us are very perceptive. Some of us are not perceptive at all. And some of us think we are perceptive when actually we are cynical or just plain touchy, reading in hidden meanings that aren't there at all.

In either type of communication—symbolic or empathic—we make ourselves known to each other in greater or lesser degrees. We use a slang term for it. We say "he comes on strong" and we mean he has an overpowering personality, be it good or bad; or "he comes on weak," whatever the case may be.

Sometimes we just don't "come on" at all. This puts me in mind of a little fellow who was performing with his primary group for Children's Day. They were portraying Christ's healing of the blind man. They were all dressed in robes, and they had headpieces held in place by men's neckties. This little chap marched up to the one playing the Lord, but just before he got there, his necktie slipped down over his eyes, and in his confusion he faced *away* from the "Lord" and cried, "Lord, I cannot see!" He was in there trying, but he'd got it all

171

hopelessly mixed up, and didn't "come on."

Sometimes we "come on" too strong. In this same performance, only this time a group was depicting the healing of Peter's mother, another little chap marched onto the stage and muttered something we could not hear at all. He had stopped about four feet short of the mike. The teacher got up from her seat in the front row, crouched in front of the platform and with small "pssst's" gestured for him to come closer to the mike. He did. He put his mouth about an eighth of an inch from it and screamed, "MY MOTHER-IN-LAW IS SICK!" It is not too much of an exaggeration to say he nearly blew us out of the back of the church.

Both of these catastrophies were taken graciously by the audience. On Children's Day, there was always a request printed in bold type on the church calendar: "Please do not laugh at the children's mistakes. They are taking their performances very seriously. You can do untold harm." We laughed only in retrospect. And with tenderness.

Sometimes we are a bit slow to make our point. Someone asks us what time it is and before we get around to telling him, we explain how to make a watch.

I turned on the radio one morning to get the news while I was eating breakfast. Nothing happened. I turned the volume control up full. Nothing happened. So I just left it that way and went on with the business of eating. About five minutes later I had some scrambled eggs halfway to my mouth, when suddenly, full blast, the radio shrieked at me "YOU'LL WONDER WHERE THE YELLOW WENT—!" I was scraping scrambled eggs off the walls for a week.

Sometimes we communicate our feelings without thinking. It's like a reflex action. Out of the horrendous Bel Air Fire in Los Angeles came some of the most heartbreaking tales—of immense courage and sometimes of appalling callousness on the part of sightseers who obstructed traffic and prevented fire equipment from getting through. But there is one comicotragic tale that sticks in my mind. A woman broke away from those who were trying to restrain her, ran madly into her fiercely burning house and came back out with, of all things—a book of blue chip stamps. Now admittedly she was in a state of shock so I am not being entirely fair to her. It is hard to believe that a book of blue chip stamps was that important to her. But shock or no, she communicated her feelings by reflex action.

I reacted reflexly once in a most peculiar manner too. I was at a conference in the San Bernardino mountains. It was afternoon and I had spoken that morning and so a nice siesta seemed in order. I was right in the midst of this most pleasant pastime when a jet plane came through the canyon between two snowcapped mountains and broke the sound barrier. Those were the days when sonic booms were rare, and you've never heard one anyhow until you've heard it reverberating through those canyons and ricocheting along the rocks. I thought the very mountains were tumbling down. I literally did. I leapt from my bed, dashed out of my cabin and ran a few feet, then came to a skidding stop, my arms outstretched, my head flung back—and shouted

"OH GOD HOW GREAT THOU ART!"

I actually thought the Lord had come!*

I had done this entirely without thinking; it had been pure reflex. When I realized it was a sonic boom I crept sheepishly back to my cabin and vowed never to tell a soul. Indeed I did not, for many years.

Well, in view of all this, how should we communicate? Symbolic or empathic, what should our manner of communication be?

I was walking back to the hotel from the Billy

*And I wanted him to know whose side I was on.

174

Sunday Tabernacle at Winona Lake one night and I ran into a group of people. They greeted me, introduced themselves, and we started to chat. Alongside were two little girls with lollipops. While we talked our grown-up talk, they stood there with solemn eyes, nursing their lollipops with the patience well-trained little girls have when they realize their parents are stuck with some idiot and they just have to wait.

We talked on and on. But suddenly the man turned to his daughters and said, "Do you know all the story records you have? Well *this* is the lady who tells the stories!"

Well!

Their lollipops went crashing to the pavement. They leapt upon me with leaps that would have qualified them for the standing broad jump in the Olympics. One of them leapt to my chest, embracing me around my neck; the other one leapt to my knees and embraced me around my middle. "Ohhhhhhh-UMMMMMMPH!" they both squealed. "Ohhhhhh-UMMMPH!" I came back, getting into the spirit of the thing.

We communicated. On several different levels of awareness, all the stops pulled out.

Now I do not recommend that we go about jumping up on people. But we can ask God to help us to communicate with the ingenuousness of a child, without guile, in all honesty, as far as we are capable of being honest.

Communication is one of the most priceless gifts God has given us. We take it for granted, distort it and abuse it; how often does it occur to thank God

175

for it? Without it we would not be able to get along in life.

One of the most pathetic sights I have ever seen was a young girl in a psychiatric ward who just sat and stared. You could put her in any position, even an uncomfortable one, and she would stay that way until she was moved again. Or pass a lighted match in front of her eyes, close enough to nearly singe the lashes and there would be absolutely no reaction. She had crawled way down inside somewhere and locked herself in and she was incapable of communicating with anyone.

I was on a plane once that could not land because there was a small private plane lost somewhere in the foggy sky outside our windows and we circled and circled, waiting for the radio tower to establish contact with little plane's pilot and guide him safely down. After awhile we landed with no further word about its whereabouts. When I got to my hotel room I turned on TV to get the news. The little plane's communication system had failed, and it had crashed, lost and alone in the fog.

This ability to communicate is something to reckon with; it can serve us well when we play the ground rules properly. The problems we can cause by abusing it are appalling. The idea of losing it altogether is something to give us pause, thank God for it, and vow never to take it for granted again.

**Just talking
and listening**

Now ALL this business of expressing ourselves to others and telling them what we mean and understanding others and what they mean and understanding ourselves and what *we* mean is carrying things just about far enough. But to drag in feeling tones and levels of awareness and attitudes in all their bewildering complexities is just too *much*. "In the name of common sense," we wail, "All we want to do is talk to people and listen to people and make friends and go hear good speakers and work in our business and in our church and carry on a normal uncomplicated life. Do we have to turn ourselves inside out to do it? Why all this introspection? What about just nice normal conversation?"

All right.

THE ART OF CONVERSATION

Conversation is "the interchange of ideas and information." Unfortunately this definition has been watered down and twisted around to suit our needs until, almost universally, we accept the definition that conversation is "the art of talking." And we get

And we get a bit fuzzy about who is supposed to be talking.

a bit fuzzy about who is supposed to be talking and naturally we conclude that it is we who are, and so we talk. And talk. And talk. If we are ever chided for it afterward we say plaintively, "Well I *did* stop— and then there was this dreadful silence and nobody seemed able to bring up anything else, so I just felt I *had* to go on." Actually we left everybody in a state of shock or apathy or resignation; they'd just "tuned out" and decided it was no use saying anything anyhow, they might as well give up. Any thoughts they'd marshalled or any ideas they'd had, had long since withered on the vine. And we go home perfectly happy in the fact that we are absolutely the last word in the art of conversation, and what on earth would everybody have done anyhow, if we hadn't kept things going? And some of us go on this way to the end, never knowing that the art of conversation is an *interchange*, not a monologue.

Conversation is the art of talking at the right time. The right time can best be distinguished by stating when the right time is *not*. The right time is not when the meeting is assembling or a class is beginning or the organ is playing the prelude before church. Or in a busy office. Or when your companion's children are clamoring for attention. Or when her husband has just come home. Or when the waitress is due any moment to take your order and you haven't opened the menu yet. Or when the motor is running and your victim is obviously champing at the bit, waiting to get out of the car and get home, or let *you* out so he can get home. Or when the person you phoned is obviously preoccupied and you have been an interruption. Or when beautiful music is playing. Or when a fiery sunset is melding with the sea. (The only thing you may talk about at a time like this is love. Any kind. If you talk about anything else you deserve to talk to yourself for the rest of your life.)

Conversation is the art of talking on an acceptable topic. An acceptable topic is not the other person's age or why he never married or his financial status or the personal aspects of his job, his boss or associates, or any scandal about *anybody*. I chided a man once about his wife and gleefully accused him of chaining her to the sink; why wasn't she here? He grinned and admitted that he did chain her to the sink while he traveled, and everyone laughed and joined in the sport. I learned later that his wife had left him and his heart was broken and his life was shattered through no fault of his own. I was numb with regret that I had been

181

so crass. Tread carefully upon other people's personal lives; you may be treading upon something very painful. And none of your business.

Acceptable topics are topics of mutual interest. And what are topics of mutual interest? The things the other fellow is interested in, if you're smart.

A few rare souls are born with the art of listening.

THE ART OF LISTENING

A few rare souls are born with the art of listening built in. The rest of us have to develop it, for the truth of the matter is that we would rather talk than listen any day. We would deny it to the end. We ask the other fellow all about himself and, "Uh huh, uh huh, uh huh," we say and hurry on to our next question, rushing him through and then when we've gotten all that out of the way, we settle down to telling him about ourselves, saving the best part till last. We console ourselves that we've already listened to *him*, when in fact we have just got all the possible interruptions taken care of so we are free now to have the stage. And yet, in this business of getting along with others, a greater part of our time ought to be consumed in listening.

Our early training doesn't help. From the beginning reading and writing are emphasized and speaking and listening are neglected, and the more we advance into modern communication the more visuals are stressed. Our educators hit us over the head with visual communication until we do not need to hear anything anymore.

Tests from a large Midwestern university have revealed some interesting facts about listening, at different ages. In these tests, the teacher suddenly interrupted her teaching and asked: "What was I talking about?" And "What were you thinking about?" In the lower grades the answers were verbal and recorded on tape. In the upper grades the answers were written and not signed.

Ninety percent of first graders were listening. Eighty percent of second graders were listening. Then the percentage tapered off. Forty-three percent of Junior Highs were listening. And twenty percent of the High Schoolers were listening. The older we get the more we have on our minds to keep us from listening. And the fact that most of us weren't taught proper habits to begin with compounds the problem.

Sales surveys are educated guesses at best because people seldom say what they mean. But sales surveys consistently turn up the fact that among lost customers, the movers and the floaters and the chronic gripers and the cheaper-price-seekers are very few. Most customers leave because the sales people are indifferent to their needs; they don't listen. One of Cornelia Otis Skinner's most hilarious skits concerns her misadventures in a large department store where she goes for a box of face powder. She is shifted about from department to department and winds up meekly going through a reducing treatment in the Beauty Salon, all the while protesting, "But all I wanted was a box of face powder."

Regardless of our age, most of us listen as we were taught in early school years.

We are more gullible when we listen than when we read. When we read we can evaluate, go back over it if we are confused, get it straight at last. But in listening we are prey to all the pitfalls; the sorrowful eyes and the dulcet voice, or the sparkling eyes and the enthusiastic voice. And in either case, the expressive face. The color of verbal expression can trip us up.

A producer wanted to know about my script for a TV shot once, and I started to tell him. "Don't *tell* me," he moaned. "If you tell me I might think it's good and it may not be good at all. Send me a script and let me read it for myself." He was a shrewd man. He knew he could read more accurately than he could listen.

It is not just that we are easily duped when we listen; we dupe ourselves. If we have any doubts about this, the famous program "Invasion from Mars" should put us in our place. To begin with, the program carried careful announcements that it was only a story, not a fact. But newspaper accounts tell us that about a million people did not hear anything but the word "Invasion."

Twenty families in a single block in Newark rushed to the street, their faces covered with wet

It was hours before the panic could be quelled.

towels. They thought it was a gas raid. In Mt. Vernon, New York, a man who had been a hopeless invalid for years rushed from his home, climbed into his auto and disappeared. The phone companies' switchboards were flooded with more calls than they could handle—people phoning other people to say I'm sorry and I wish I had and it's too late now and I love you or whatever the case might be, and farewell forever. Orson Welles and his cast looked up from their scripts to find the control room in their studio full of police.

It was hours before the panic could be quelled, and it was not until the next morning that a nation looked abash at the repercussions in the morning papers. It seems ridiculous, but it happened.

I had a little story once called "I Haven't Time" about a mother who did not have time for her son until he was killed in a car accident. It had such an emotional impact whenever I told it that I decided to explain before I began that it was pure fiction. But to no avail. More often than not, someone would come up to me afterward, wringing my hands in sympathy.

We "tune out" to avoid difficult listening. Some of us actually brag about it. "I can look a person right in the eye and never hear a word he says." We "turn our hearing aids off" and go off into lapses, taking our own flights of fancy or going on with what we were thinking about before this person interrupted our thoughts, and coming back with the appropriate "uh huh's" at proper intervals. In order to do this we develop the habit of "faking attention." Some of us do it well from long practice; others of us don't fool anybody.

Our reasons for doing this are legion. We are threatened or affronted, or what is being said is not pleasant or acceptable, or the person talking is a crashing bore. Whatever our reasons, we are the losers. For we miss gems of learning, of understanding, of correction, of new ideas, that may never come our way again. Listening consumes energy. *Our* energy. To "turn our hearing aids off" is the lazy way out.

We are influenced by the person we are listening to. This is made glaringly manifest in our reaction to public figures. It is, indeed, a most important factor in vote decisions, a fact well known and played upon by the "Image makers." How did he bring up his children, is he a success, is he married, is he divorced, how much influence does he have, does he have charm—these are the things that influence us, and we listen to him or "tune him out," as the case may be, depending upon how he impresses us as a person.

186

We are influenced by personal appearance. I knew a woman once who always wore the same suit on the platform. She had the unshakable conviction that what she had to say was more important than how she looked. The suit had been cleaned so many times it was threadbare but at all costs she wanted to avoid criticism. So, clean and neat, she always appeared in that same suit. Then she overheard the remark, "If she wears that grey suit once more I'll die." She wore no makeup. And then she overheard the remark, "I wish she'd use some powder; her face is so shiny I can't get my mind on what she's saying." So her unshakable convictions became a bit shakey and she bought a pink suit and a blue suit and a green suit and began to use discreet makeup. Then a little boy went up to her and said, "My mother says you use makeup." Then she overheard someone say, "She certainly has enough *clothes*." And she decided that some people were going to be influenced by her appearance if she looked one way and some people were going to be influenced by her appearance if she looked another way, and she could not please them all. So she went back to concentrating on what she had to *say*, reasoning that if she was clean and neat it did not matter which color suit she had on.

I walked out of an auditorium once after hearing a woman whose message had stirred me to the depths of my being. I had hardly seen *her*; I just wanted to get alone and think about what she had said. But in the lobby I overheard two women talking about her. One of them said, "I think she is doing something to her hair."

We yield all too easily to distractions. This is especially true in listening to public speakers. The mike is wrong and his voice is mushed. We are in a draft. It's too hard to hear. The ushers buzz about. There are children in the audience, drooling down our backs. Latecomers are crawling over us or wandering up and down the aisles. It's too stuffy— why doesn't somebody open some windows? There's a siren outside. People are whispering behind us.

I remember once, in a large auditorium, right in the middle of a discourse where I was using an illustration of Elijah's being fed by the ravens—a bat flew into the audience. He swooped, he swayed, he danced, he executed all of his most polished pirouettes—it was the ultimate in ballet. And the audience stooped and ducked and screamed and did all of the things people do when they are encountered by a bat. After a few moments I'd either had enough or was desperate—I'll never know which—I leaned against the side of the podium and said laconically, "Well I brought my own visual aids; that is one of the ravens." And with understandable relief they laughed and the panic subsided and I went matter-of-factly back to my story, both inviting and demanding that they come back down to business now, and no nonsense. The bat either got the message or was insulted at being called a raven; he promptly flew out one of the back doors.

But we yield to distractions in private listening, too. There are too many phone calls. Or other interruptions. Or our informer doodles on a pad. There may not be a bat. But we can always blame it on something. We can always find a reason why we are just *not listening.*

We can lick distractions. We can mentally shut them out. We can if we try.

We can lick
distractions
if we try.

We listen through our own emotional filters. It is well to remember this. What someone is saying and what we are hearing may be two entirely different things. They are telling us one thing and we can be listening to quite another, depending upon what is on our mind at the time. I remember a message I gave that ended with the challenge: "Arise and be doing. Do it *now.*" I gave it on the radio once and a boy wrote me that he had decided to become a priest. I gave it on a platform once and a woman told me afterward that she had decided to divorce her husband.

The odds are against us. The art of listening isn't easy. We have to listen to people whose thoughts are totally disorganized, to people who do not look at us while they are speaking, to people who keep saying "Do you see? Do you see?" when we not only see but are ten minutes ahead of them and have already smelled out the denouement, to people who answer our questions before we ask them

189

("Oh," you ask, "why do I think this? Well I'll tell you why I think this—"), to people who are saying one thing and meaning another, to people who speak in pious platitudes and vague spiritual generalities without ever getting down to cases, to people who speak so low or so rapidly that we can only guess what they're saying—

No it isn't easy. But the responsibility of listening is ours. And it is a lonely business; no one else is going to help us.

The least we can do is not compound the error and pass the same problems on to our children. How wonderful to start practicing the art of listening in the home. How fortunate the children who can sit at the dinner table while *everyone* in the family tells a bit of what he did and thought that day—with everybody listening! Children need to both talk and listen. They are feeling their way into the realm of ideas. How we listen to them determines how they will listen to others.

**All the rules
are in one word**

LOVE GOES DOWN to the very bones. Literally. Its deprivation can not only cause children to be dwarfed emotionally (we already know this) but physically as well. For some love-starved children have been known to stop growing in spite of enormous—and weird—appetites (they steal from the refrigerator, from the dog's plate and even out of the garbage) and abnormal thirst (they drink water from puddles and even from the toilet bowl). It is called "deprivation dwarfism." A tiny center in the brain that controls bone growth goes berserk. But when they are placed in love-filled homes, they shoot up to normal growth in an amazingly short time, with no special treatment. "Surely," say the medical reports, "love must be more than skin-deep when its absence can turn off vital centers of the brain, and its presence can turn them back on again." The power of love is staggering to contemplate.

The rules are good to know. And it is true that if we know them we are jogged up a bit and God has more to work with. But they are only guideposts. All the rules are embodied in love. The beginning and the middle and the end—is love.

Though I go forth in the glamour of the public eye and sway people by my oratory and dialectic and vast knowledge of Scripture or Christian Education, or thrill them with my singing or my ability to execute a musical instrument to perfection, and go home and gripe because my family does not say "how high?" when I say "jump," I am just a great big noise.

And though I can delve into the mysteries and secret truths of God, and have such faith that I earn myself a reputation of a remover of mountains, and do not even try to understand the frustrations and loneliness of my dear ones and co-workers, or try to remove the mountains of misunderstanding between us, I am a great big zero.

And though I am renowned as a tither and a giver to missions, or even offer to go myself, much to the praise and approbation of all who know me, and shut myself off from people right under my nose when they ask for a moment of my time or a smidgen of my understanding, I am a great big loser.

Love lasts and lasts when there is nothing any longer to feed it, stays on fire when no one is around to stoke the furnace, is patient with the patience that defies all onslaughts of criticism and indifference and lack of appreciation, and is kind.

Love never longs after or begrudges the excellence or good fortune of others, nor boils over with jealousy of their ability or popularity; does not boast or become unduly elated over its own attainments, makes no parade, gives itself no airs. It is not conceited or inflated, does not consider itself above the hoi polloi, does not go about reminding others that it is the boss and will take no nonsense and wants no suggestions, does not forget that Scripture is replete with the reminder that "God raised himself up another."

It is not rude or unmannerly, forgetting to put the other person's feelings first, and does not blow a gasket every time it is provoked.

Love does not fight for its rights or its own way, either by pounding desks or speaking in low measured tones or lining up allies for the battle—for it is not self-seeking.

Love is not touchy and does not take every chance remark personally or imagine everyone is plotting against it. It is not fretful or sniping or complaining or resentful, expressing indignant displeasure at every imagined wrong with "righteous indignation." It takes no account of the evil done to it—does not brood over it and nurse it and keep it alive, boring everyone stiff with repeated accounts of it.

Love does not smack its lips over scandal or backsliding of others even under the guise of "talking about it so we can pray more intelligently"— but rejoices when right and truth prevail, not saying, "Well I'm glad she finally straightened out—it's about *time*."

Love bears up under anything and everything

195

that comes, without bellowing about it loud and clear to all who are within hearing; is ever ready to believe the best about every person. It is incurably optimistic under all circumstances, looking on the bright side, knowing God is still in heaven and perfectly capable no matter how things look. And it endures everything, not with a helpless sigh of self-pity or a wan smile or a grim stiff upper lip that casts a pall of gloom over everyone who comes near ("I'll endure this if it kills me!")—but with a calm and cheerful strength that defies pity and makes onlookers take courage and draw strength.

Love never fails—never fades out or becomes old-fashioned and never comes to an end. As for prophecy, the uncertain tomorrows will become certain yesterdays and go down as history as time goes inexorably on. As for knowledge, it will lose its value and be superseded by truth. For our knowledge is fragmentary, incomplete and imperfect.

But when the total complete and perfect truth comes—and God has promised that it will—all the incomplete and imperfect will vanish away. But one thing will not vanish away.

Love.

It is here to stay.

And it leaves no room for coddling past mistakes, either others or our own. "... forgetting those things which are behind, and reaching forth unto those things which are before, I press toward the mark for the prize of the high calling of God in Christ Jesus." Or, as Phillips puts it: "... I *leave the past behind* and with hands outstretched to whatever lies ahead—I go straight for the goal...."

We who are spiritual

"WHAT ROT, these rules," we cry. "The whole secret is complete dependence upon the Holy Spirit and constant communion with God."

We mean it. We preach it to all who will listen. We preach it and preach it and preach it. And we go off to meditate and re-evaluate ourselves and our relationship with God. This is good. The crux is not *that* we do it; the crux is *when* we do it. For the problem is that often while we are thus busily engaged others may have to do the job at hand that God has assigned us to do.

There was a boy in an organization once who missed the crux. He was fresh from Bible school and working in the stock room for the summer. And he had Thomas Aquinas and Andrew Murray and the Bible propped open on the shelves, and plaques and reminders all over his working area so that he could keep on being spiritual and show others that he surely was. The only problem was that he never got his work done. Whenever a rush order was in the offing, he was always off having devotions. And he would come back, dewy-eyed, after others had done his job, and tell everyone of the new revelation he'd just had from God, and look at them with sorrowful eyes, grieved that they did not comprehend the deeper things, the important things, that somehow he had managed to find out and to practice.

He was fired.

And he went on his way, patient and loving toward those who had thus persecuted him "for righteousness sake," spiritual to the end.

And a man in a minor executive position who spent his days on the phone, counseling, admonishing, setting up meetings concerning the deeper things of God, and discussing at great length spiritual things with his secretary and calling special prayer meetings. The only problem was that he never got his work done. Whenever a deadline was in the offing, he was always off having devotions.

He was fired.

And he went on his way patient and loving toward those who had thus persecuted him "for righteousness sake" and spiritual to the end.

And a woman who spent her days and nights in meditation on the deeper things of God, and mooched all her meals from friends, dropping in without warning, saying wanly that she was "really not very hungry, she was so worn out with all this meditation," (and eating everything in sight) and saying constantly that "The Lord would provide," and declining to help with the dishes afterward because she was so exhausted with all this delving into the more spiritual things that others seemed to have had no time for.

There are others. And the chances are they go through life failing in their jobs, in their human relationships everywhere, and wondering why nobody else seems to grasp the deeper things that they have grasped.

There was a woman whose life was suddenly in shambles one night, broken in a million pieces at her feet. But there were two small boys running toy motor cars across the kitchen floor and quarreling over who had the right of way, and there was a cat between her feet purring and rubbing against her ankles and there was a puppy jumping up and making runs in her stockings and clamoring to be fed. She could have called in neighbors or friends to weep on or gone off and had devotions or preached to the two small boys, but instead she thought "Peel the potatoes." Now why such a singularly unspiritual thought should have come to her mind she would never know, but it did. Of course there was more to it than that. She had to fix the meat too and the vegetables, and straighten out the boys and feed the puppy and get that crazy cat from between her ankles before she tripped and broke her neck. But she knew that she had to somehow do all these things, that indeed if she had any personal relationship with God and knew anything about the deeper secrets of his love, this was the time to put it all into practice.

So they had their meal and they had a joyful grace and a lively conversation and good laughter to go with it. The puppy slept in a corner. And the cat slept on the window sill. And the boys got put to bed with confidence in God and they never suspected their lives were in shambles.

This woman knew God was with her with every breath she drew; that he knew, that he cared, that he would tell her exactly what to do next, no more, just that, and she would trust him for the rest.

And afterward she went to him, knelt for hours listening to him.

If indeed we have this deeper spiritual communication with God, if we know him in our quiet hours, if we have really appropriated his deeper truths into our lives, then they are in us, in our very living and breathing, always, in all things, and we don't have to go about expounding; we *live* them with every breath we draw. We do the job—not with a martyr-like and dignified acquiescence, feeling terribly spiritual all the while, but with a down-to-earth practicality, knowing that the job must get done.

We work it out in secret with him; he works it out in practical ways with us. And we do not go about preaching what he has revealed to us; we go about *doing* it.

Paul knew this. He preached, all right. But he also made tents.

Don't take yourself
too seriously

THIS IS AN AREA in which you will have a great deal of help, for the moment you forget and begin to take yourself seriously there is always some good brother or sister to come to the rescue and put you back on the right path again.

I discovered this once when I expressed my appreciation to a friend in a moment of out-goingness. I had left her in no doubt of it, down through the years, but this was one of those warm impulses and I quite outdid myself; I delivered a veritable panegyric and thanked her for everything she was and did and threw in a few things she was not and didn't. "I love you too, dearie," she said, "and I thank you for—thank you for—" she was struggling valiantly, groping for it as if rummaging in a drawer through a jumble of old socks. *I* was struggling too, with mental telepathy, trying to help her. I could think of a hundred things she could thank me for. But she wasn't getting the message. "I thank you for—" she said again, desperately. And at last she found it, pulled it out and held it aloft in triumph—"for teaching me to wear rubber gloves when I do dishes."

"Thanks a *lot*," I said.

"It was the only thing I could *think* of," she said plaintively.

Well I had to admit she was really in there, trying.

I discovered it again once, when I was speaking at a banquet. After I started to speak I noticed that a gentleman was taping me. My secretary always wrote ahead that I was not to be taped, but the wires had got crossed somewhere. I did not want to embarrass him so I went on speaking with the idea that I would straighten it out later. After I finished, a popular recording-artist and ex-actor closed with some songs. It turned out that he had considerable to say in between his songs, and it took an hour before he was finally depleted and emptied of everything he had to say and to sing. After it was all over and while the audience was sleeping, I went up to the gentleman who was taping me and explained very diplomatically that it was not allowed.

"Well it's okay," he said. "Because I started to tape X—"

"Yes?"

"But he went on and on—"

"And?"

"Well I ran out of tape—"

"Yes?"

"And I wiped you off."

"Oh."

"So there's no problem."

"No," I said, "there's no problem."

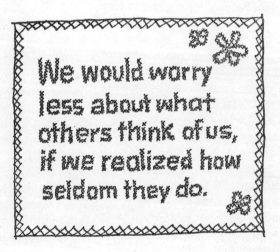

We would worry less about what others think of us, if we realized how seldom they do.